Copyright © 2019 Jacob DeNeui All Rights Reserved
No part of this publication may be reproduced, distributed, or transmitted in any form or by any means, including photocopying, recording, or other electronic or mechanical methods, without the prior written permission of the author, except in the case of brief quotations embodied in reviews and certain other non-commercial uses permitted by copyright law.

Graphics by Jacob DeNeui and David Yakos
Book cover design by Jacob DeNeui

ISBN: 9781795232944

DESIGN
BEFORE YOU
DESIGN

HOW ORGANIZATION INNOVATION

CAN EMPOWER SOCIAL ENTREPRENEURSHIP

Check out my BLOG!

It's where I share my ideas on design, leadership, and social impact.

And it's FREE!

www.jacobideas.com/blog

CONTENTS

Preface	1-2
Introduction	3-16
Chapter 1: Adventure Begins	17-31
Chapter 2: The Struggle Is Real	32-52
Case Study: Tegu	53-57
Chapter 3: Innovate or Die	58-76
Chapter 4 Bird's Eye View	77-94
Case Study: Cold Smoke Coffeehouse	95-99
Chapter 5: Pickle Ice Cream Sundae	100-128
Chapter 6: You Do You, Boo	129-148
Case Study: Sseko Designs	149-153
Chapter 7: Show Me the Money	154-186
Chapter 8: Harder, Better, Faster, Stronger	187-212
Conclusion	213-220
Acknowledgments	221-222
Glossary	223-226
Bibliography	227-237

PREFACE

*"Every child is an artist. The problem is
how to remain an artist
once we grow up."*
- Pablo Picasso

I wanted to be Spider-Man's Ben Parker or Luke Skywalker's Yoda. I wanted to encourage other designers like myself to use their powers for good, not vain ambition. What was born from that desire was my first attempt at a book which I creatively titled *Entrepreneurship in Non-Profit Architecture*.

Sounds thrilling, I know.

It's the kind of book you read late at night when even NyQuil has failed to put you to sleep. (If you're searching for it on Amazon, don't hold your breath).

However, I couldn't escape the passion I felt for harnessing the power of creativity for social impact. As C. S. Lewis put it, "I was with book, as a woman is with child." I've had some incredible dabbles into the world of social impact design (a term I'll break down in the Introduction), and they all served to wet my appetite for more. It was largely through these experiences that I realized there must be more that design could do to help solve the world's huge problems: physical and spiritual depravity, environmental desecration, violence and devastation.

Four years later, I began the process of creating this book, *Design Before You Design: How Organization Innovation Can Empower Social Entrepreneurship*. Yes, the title might lead you to believe that the book is only for architects and the artsy-fartsy designer types that draw expensive fur coats and wear what you swear are clothes sewn from fabric ripped straight off your grandmother's old floral couch. But I wrote this book for the **social entrepreneur** seeking **fresh inspiration and ideation** on how to **design their organization** in order to **maximize their impact**. Even if *you* don't consider yourself a "designer" or "artist," I do!

I believe with every fiber of my being that we are all designers created to actively participate in the joy of making a better world. From the sixteen-year-old with hopes of improving child care to the robotics engineer working to give life-bringing technology to developing nations, we are many who feel the burden of social entrepreneurship*[1].

In my delightful love affair with design, I've found her to be far more than mere eye candy. She holds the incredible power to transform how we view the world, how we perceive problems, and hence, how we solve those problems. This book shares my lover's secret gifts with the rest of the world. (Did I take the metaphor too far?). As you read it, I hope you will discover new and exciting ways to don the goggles of design in your approach to social entrepreneurship so that your creative genius might be inspired and perhaps softly whisper to you new ideas and revelations about your own social venture.

Let's begin.

---

1 * Indicates a word defined in the Glossary beginning on page 223

INTRODUCTION

*"We are the music-makers,
And we are the dreamers of dreams,
Wandering by lone sea-breakers,
And sitting by desolate streams.
World-losers and world-forsakers,
Upon whom the pale moon gleams;
Yet we are the movers and shakers,
Of the world forever, it seems."*
                          - Arthur O'Shaughnessy

People matter.

Philosophy and theology write books, creeds, and mantras to understand and describe this belief but it is the undying song of humanity that perhaps proclaims this truth the loudest in a chorus that has resonated harmoniously throughout empires and societies since time began.

People matter.

What a simple statement, yet upon its shoulders empires have risen and fallen, beauty has been created and distorted, and paradigms formed and negated.

Charles Dickens is credited with stating that "no one is useless in this world who lightens the burden of it to anyone else," a profound declaration which leaves us face to face with this simple truth: we humans need each other.

It's no secret that the world around us is changing—and it is changing fast. We live in the dawn of the Information Age*, a time of incredible break-neck speed advancement in technology and understanding of the world we live in. Despite the overtly pessimistic agenda that oozes from most news organizations, innovative tools and ideas are being employed in the quest to sing out in harmony with humanity's song of equality. Across numerous industries and fields, mankind's worth is continually reinforced through these breakthroughs as the fruits of innovation are distributed to meet our greatest needs.

Over the past thirty years, poverty has decreased by an incredible 73 percent. In addition, the world has seen the number of ongoing wars drop by 50 percent, there are now 30 percent less autocracies and 83 percent less nuclear weapons.[1] Artificial intelligence is beginning to aid medicine in helping doctors diagnose diseases. Increased global interconnectedness is helping organizations combat the growing slave industry across the world.

Yet despite these incredible victories, we continue to come head to head with adversity, both external and internal. In 2013, more than 700 million people lived in poverty.[2] In 2017, five countries were engaged in armed conflicts that killed more than 10,000 people, and fifty-five were engaged in conflicts that killed 10,000

---

1 Pinker. "Is the World Getting Better."
2 Carnoy and Garcia. "Five Key Trends."

or less.[3] Twenty-one countries with populations greater than half a million are ruled by a single person with absolute power.[4] There are nearly 15,000 known nuclear warheads across the world ready to be deployed. More than three million people die each year from preventable diseases, half of them being five years or younger.[5] In 2016, more than forty million people were estimated to be victims of slavery, 10 million of them being children.[6]

Assumption
Herein lies the problem: Global suffering and inequality continue to go largely unresolved while we, social entrepreneurs, hold untapped potential to create solutions. Since I know you're an intelligent person—you are, after all, reading my book—it probably won't take you long to note that this book will not go into detail about such suffering and inequality. To describe the origins and details of this suffering and inequality would be too extensive and detract from the objective. That's why we are going to carry on under the mutual assumption that these exist.

The Unopened Gift
Thankfully, we have been offered gifts and resources such as education, law, medicine, and technology that have helped combat the damaging effects of these forces. In the words of Nelson Mandela, "Education is the most powerful weapon you can use to change the world." Many social entrepreneurs have done an inspiring job of leading the way by utilizing these gifts, and for that they are all to be commended.

3 Wikipedia. "List of Ongoing Armed Conflicts."
4 Desilver. "Despite Concerns about Global Democracy."
5 Offit. "Global Immunization."
6 "Global Estimates on Modern Slavery."

However, there is one resource we have been afforded that has more often than not been left out of the conversation: **design.***

As we journey together, we will unpack how social entrepreneurs can utilize the power of design thinking in response to the specific need they see in the world which they feel burdened to address, specifically through the "turbo-powered-rocket booster-jet-pack" of innovation.*

La Femme Fatale
I'm an architect, which means I'm a designer. Ever since I was old enough to ponder my future, I can always remember imagining the world as a better place. (I mean seriously, how could lightsabers and Jedi NOT add to the thriving of human civilization?) Later, however, my design mindset shifted to thoughts on how my friends and I could help my neighbors with their chores. This shift culminated in the creation of what I fondly called the "Helpers Club," my attempt to forcefully wrangle my friends into helping our neighbors pull a couple of weeds (needless to say it didn't last long). Along my designer journey, my mind spent serious time considering

the possibility of designing a super legit underground mansion which I would, of course, build beneath my super legit mansion. These thoughts and desires are what insatiably drew me to architecture and my undying love for design and creativity.*

But as I began to pursue my lovely career choice, I also saw architecture's more undesirable characteristics. Sure, she looked amazing! She was bold and creative. No one with even the slightest bit of good taste could keep from gawking at her and all her immaculate details, crisp lines, and of course, glass (the material all architect teenage dreams are made of).

However, while magazines became saturated with her images and words of praise oozed from the mouths of star struck critics, I couldn't help but pull my gaze aside and notice "the others." You know, the shabbily dressed, lifeless boxes that housed the world's greatest needs. Their poorly thought out crusty façades reflected the lack of love they received from the world around them. And as my eyes shifted from the beauty to the beast, I couldn't help but question what economic or cultural forces had so directed this scene, this dichotomy that now assaulted my mind.

Whether you're an architect or not, it's probably a safe bet to guess that you've seen what I'm talking about, even if it was in a different scenario. Perhaps it was when you discovered that the odds of African American students in America obtaining adequate math and reading levels was significantly lower than that of white children.[7] Maybe it was after you visited sub-Saharan Africa and were introduced to that gorgeous, innocent baby girl whose odds of dying before the age of five were fifteen times as high as those born

7 Carnoy

in your friendly neighborhood.[8] The sad truth is that if our eyes have been opened to the world around us, we have seen this disparity. We have seen the best of our finances, time, and effort given to those most capable of providing compensation for those services.

    This is basic economics, and I am by no means insinuating that it should be abandoned or manipulated! What I am proposing is that, in the spirit of this book, we, the world changers, have the power to rewrite the narrative of our reality through design. One person described design as the transformation of existing conditions into more desirable ones. Through this book, I hope to share how design can not only influence the quality of space people inhabit but can also transform the current conditions of the industry or vocation that has grabbed your attention and turn them into more desirable ones.

Double Duty
The field of design will function two-fold for us: first and foremost, we will see how all social entrepreneurs can harness design **thinking** as a tool for creating innovative solutions to the formation of their organizations. Second, we will explore the realm of "**social impact design**"* (we'll call it SID for short) in order to see how controlled amounts of innovation within a field (more on this in Chapter 6) is connected to that field's effectiveness. By exploring this niche sector of social impact work, we will better understand both the need for social entrepreneurs to innovate in how they form their organizations while simultaneously discovering how some designers are using their creative gifts for the advancement of their work.

8 "Children: Reducing Mortality"

SID

But before we begin using SID as our precedent, let's start by making sure we all understand what it even is. This altruistic application of design goes by many names: impact design, social design, humanitarian design,* public interest design, and others. They're all great terms, but for clarity's sake it is important to have a consistent working definition. I chose the term *social impact design* to describe the use of design for specifically "social" or "altruistic" causes. While most of us likely have a certain degree of understanding about what this term means, numerous other terms have been coined to describe this idea which is why I find it important to take some time to explain the rationale behind why I chose to use it in lieu of others.

For the purposes of this book, we will define SID to mean the following:

> "Altruistic design that creates positive change by respecting the dignity and value of all mankind."

Allow me to further explain the intentional use of each of these three words: social, impact, and design.

Why "Social"?

One of the ways Webster's dictionary defines the word *social* is "the welfare of human beings as members of society." In all of SID, the core belief is that regardless of race, creed, religion, or social status **people matter**. Because of this bond, the clarifying term *social* is of great value in that it provides a powerful reference point back to design's inviolable purpose of equitable application for all people.

Why "Impact"?

As a verb, *impact* is defined as "to have a strong effect on someone or something." It certainly does carry with it a strong and possibly aggressive connotation of force with it. (If someone says "3-2-1 IMPACT!" it usually means something just blew up.) The word can also be defined as "the action of one object coming forcibly into contact with another." It does all seem a bit brutish, doesn't it?

Not if you think of impact in terms of effectiveness.

Allow me to elaborate through the comparison of a drill driver vs. an impact driver. Both tools can be used to drive screws, but the impact driver has been shown to effectively double or triple the turning force of the drill driver. This is due to the fact that, on top of simple rotation, the impact driver applies concussive blows to the screw, allowing it to drive screws deeper and faster than

its well-intentioned competitor. It's one thing to lightly "influence" or "affect" social needs, but it's another to bring powerful, concussive "impact" when facing real problems that require strong and powerful solutions.

Social entrepreneurs tend to have a significant amount of piss and vinegar when it comes to how moved they are to act on social issues in the world. Just look at the story of Cameron Sinclair and the founding of Architecture for Humanity. Having been effectively fed up with a lack of action in the design world in response to humanitarian needs, he forcefully took it into his own hands to "be the change he wished to see in the world," as Gandhi once said. A drill driver wasn't enough for him. He needed an IMPACT driver.

And Design...
For the purpose of this book we will define *design* as the following:

> "The intentional process by which an original physical, digital, or intellectual product is created."

This word can be used to mean both a **process** as well as a **product**. We will primarily use the word to describe a process, though when referring to SID one can see how design as a product also applies. And because of the vastness of possible applications through which design can be utilized, I *intentionally* (see what I did there?) limited the description of the word **process** to simply **intentional**, implying that any number of descriptors, such as "creative," "careful," "logical," and/or "diligent," could be a satisfactory substitute so long as the process involved a focused effort from one's mental and/or emotional capabilities and not merely a process left to chance and circumstance. **Original** is important because it infers that the created object must be distinctly unique, otherwise the object would simply be "built" instead of "designed." The terms **physical**, **digital**, and **intellectual** imply that all of these fields contain possible applications for design, including everything from pavement on roads, a website, an oil painting, an organizational process, or a song.

Now that we have defined our terms as well as their literary subcomponents, what is the practical definition of SID? SID is **a partnership between a design field** (e.g., fashion, technology, architecture, graphic design, etc.) **and an altruistic cause** (e.g., Ugandan women's rights, environmental preservation, racial equality, etc.). SID will play an important role in our discussion of the value of design for social entrepreneurs as they form (or reform) the structure of their organization. Before launching into our ultimate goal of how to apply design in the innovation of our social impact organizations, we will start by allowing SID to show us why design, creativity, and innovation are critical if we truly believe that **people matter**.

Design, Creativity, and Innovation

Let's distinguish design, creativity, and innovation in the following ways:

- **Design** uses **creativity** to produce **subjective** benefits.

- **Creativity** is the process of conceiving new ideas through the synthesis of raw information (more in Chapter 8).
- **Innovation** uses **creativity** to produce **objective** benefits.

What do these definitions mean for us? Well for starters, design and innovation are not inherently the same. One thing they have in common, however, is they both involve creativity. While design is design whether or not the end result is an objectively positive gain for society, innovation is not. Therefore, all innovation contains design while not all design is innovative.

Say a clothing designer recognizes a need for nursing mothers who live in cold environments to have clothing that is both warm but also easily manipulated for breast feeding. Said designer researches, prototypes, and eventually creates a final product. However, despite her best efforts, the final product does not meet the original purpose of solving the problem of warm, easily manipulated clothing for nursing mothers, nor does it solve any other noteworthy need (meeting this need would have clearly been of objective benefit to nursing mothers in cold climates). However, in the process of "designing" this new idea, our designer ends up with a standard women's coat that ends up looking (at least in her eyes) more attractive than any other coat she's seen before. This is design: a new product produced through creative process with a subjective benefit to the world (beauty truly is in the eye of the beholder).

Understanding SID and how it is defined helps us understand the need for social entrepreneurs to innovate and then how to innovate. The entire premise of this book rests upon the largely untapped potential of design for social entrepreneurs to create innovation (i.e., creative and objectively positive results) within their fields in order to more fully empower their work and their cause. One might say that design is like the railroad tracks that guide and enable the engine of innovation.

The Map
Speaking of roads, I know some of us like to have an idea of where we're going ("My name is Jacob and I'm a recovering control freak"), so I thought I'd map out the rest of our journey.

In **Chapter 1**, we will introduce a fable that will help us better understand the message of the book. The fable follows a team of explorers on an uncharted island who, through an unexpected change in plans, are forced to find a solution to their problem in the best way they each see fit. I've divided the fable into three different sections (Chapters 1, 2, and 4) to give us a brief respite from the information feed while using the fable to support the book's message.

In **Chapter 2**, two of our main characters will show us what is at stake when one does not approach problems with an innovative design mindset.

Chapter 3 will elaborate on this lesson as we explore these risks with more concrete examples.

In **Chapter 4,** we will jump back to our uncharted island to see how one character successfully uses design innovation to solve the problem.

We will continue the discussion in **Chapter 5** as we explore three fundamental design tools to help you innovate your organization's design.

Finally, in **Chapters 6**, **7**, **and 8**, we will focus in on three relevant organization topics in which to utilize our newly gained tools.

And finally, between these chapters I've scattered various case studies of businesses that have incorporated innovative design principles into their structure.

Exploration
Design Before You Design is a reminder as well as a fresh outlook on design's usefulness in answering the world's deepest problems. As we look at the difference between effective vs. ineffective innovation as well as three key lessons in innovative organization design, we will see how architects, business owners, robotics engineers, and other entrepreneurs have used their design abilities to innovatively construct their business or organization model before they even started to embark on their unique work.

For too long, social entrepreneurship has largely missed out on the perks of design. It's time for social entrepreneurs to take advantage of design thinking in order to create some much-needed innovation within their work. As we look at both the problem and solution through the lens of SID, we will together explore how to apply design in the creation of any social impact organization. And where better to begin an exploration than an uncharted island...

Design is like the railroad tracks that guide and enable the engine of innovation.

Chapter 1

ADVENTURE BEGINS

*"How wonderful it
is that nobody need wait
a single moment before
starting to improve the
world."
- Ann Frank*

(12:28 PM)

Change in Plans
Sid couldn't help but stare in child-like awe as she tilted her head back to look up at the cold silver sky above. Thick, juicy snowflakes descended lazily around her, as if they had not a care in the world. It was only a brief moment she shared with those snowflakes before they joined the ranks of their companions on the snowy trail she and her team were ascending, but it was a magical one.

They had been trekking now for almost eight hours, well before the sun had risen, though they had yet to see it through all of the clouds. Cold and tired, the team drew their energy from the anticipation of summiting the island's tallest snow-covered mountain. As always, Peter had been the first one packed and ready to hit the trail running (quite literally, in his case). By 4:30 AM, the whole team was packed and ready to go.

Given the fact that their early morning expedition was starting on a sandy beach surrounded by palm trees, an outside observer might have labeled the presence of boots, parkas, and Gore-Tex gloves in their rucksacks as "overeager," but they would have been mistaken. In just a matter of hours after setting out on their trek, the team transported themselves from the sandy beach and its cool Pacific Ocean waves to a snow-laden mountain and its chilly winter winds. Sydney had read about places such as New Zealand and Chile where one could both ski and surf in the same day, but she could think of nowhere else in the world where one could reach both climates in the same day by foot.

  Yet here she stood, a mere slip and tumble away from a steep, snowy ledge overlooking some of the most majestic scenery her eyes could have ever imagined. As she beheld the incredible juxtaposition of the snowy crevasse-laden fields with the verdant greenery of the jungle just beyond, she was once again awestruck.

  Carlos had warned them yesterday evening of the dangers he predicted they might encounter today. Just two days earlier, the weather had warmed up long enough to turn the snow they saw in the distance into rain for a short time, only to be followed by a day of what they observed to be intermittent snow storms upon the mountain. He explained to them that if indeed the rain had formed a layer of ice between the two layers of snow, the circumstances were ideal for an avalanche, something nobody wanted to deal with. All morning long, Carlos had maintained a level of concern about the team's safety, constantly keeping his eyes ahead, searching for even the slightest trace of danger. So far, none had been found.

  "Sid! Watch your step girl!" Carlos's warning

snapped Sid back to reality as she hastily avoided the small ice chunk she had just about tripped over. Inside Sid cursed herself for once again getting distracted. Being one of only two females on the trip, she constantly felt the need to prove to her male teammates that she was indeed the competent, contributive member she knew herself to be. Despite her frustration, Sid was grateful for Carlos's leadership. Throughout the whole trip, he had been nothing but strong and supportive, providing encouragement when anyone felt down. He never failed to offer a helping hand to anyone on the team. Now more than ever, Sid knew all of her focus and mental toughness would be needed.

Sid, Rita, and Will all seemed confident that they would be able to avoid the chance of avalanche. Peter was skeptical. "I know Carlos seems like he knows what he's doing, Sid," Peter had said as he, Will, and Sid were almost finished tethering themselves to the rope two hours earlier to begin ascending the snowy mountain. "Just remember that not even he can stop an avalanche once it's started."

Sid fought to keep from laughing out loud. *Oh Peter, always so dramatic*, she thought. However, he did have a point, and that point was made apparent when reality reminded her just how high up she and her teammates were. One false step and—*NO, don't even go there!*—she thought, forcing her mind back to the task at hand. She looked ahead and focused on Carlos and Rita ascending the trail, ice axes in their right hands, like make-shift canes, helping to stabilize them on the somewhat tilted ledge they had been climbing for the past two hours.

Carlos stopped. As Sid, Peter, and Will caught up to the two of them, she tried to look around Rita to see what exactly Carlos was staring at. Then, turning to face the group, he said, "Team, this part of the trail here makes me a little nervous, not going to lie. It's steeper than the rest of the trail we've climbed, which makes it more likely to separate from the snow beneath it. If we proceed cautiously with our ice axes and don't make any quick moves, I think we'll be alright. Is everybody comfortable with that?"

Sid looked at Rita as she vigorously shook her head yes, then looked behind her at Will as he flashed his classic thumbs up that he loved to give so much. Peter appeared to not be as sure. She could almost see the gears spinning within his eyes as he calculated both the risk and possible reward of continuing their journey to the summit. "Well, I don't see any safer way up to the peak, so I guess let's do it," he eventually responded.

"Sid?" Carlos asked. Sid looked down the hill and back up at her courageous leader. "Let's go!" she said with more confidence than she felt. "Alright, we're on. Remember, take your time on this!" Carlos said before turning back around to face the steep ledge. Cautiously, he stretched his axe-wielding arm out, punching the snow a couple of times, before gingerly stepping his left foot onto the snow. So far so good. Slowly, he pulled up his axe and jabbed it into the snow again, this time further ahead, followed by another cautiously and carefully placed step. Rita soon followed in his footsteps, placing her own ice axe into the snow the same way. Sid, Peter, and Will observed the two as they made their way across the steep section.

Once both Carlos and Rita were close to where the trail leveled out once again, Sid began to follow. With one step at a time, she lifted her boot and jammed her jagged crampon strapped beneath it into the snow, carefully yet firmly. She did the same thing with her other foot. With Peter and Will behind her, she continued to traverse the snowy slope, occasionally feeling the teeth of her crampons sink into the ice layer buried just beneath the snowy topping.

"That's not so bad," she said between tired breaths, looking up only briefly to see Carlos and Rita smiling at her.

Before she could smile back, the twelve-inch-thick slab of snow and ice that she, Will, and Peter were on dislodged itself from rest and began hurdling itself and its passengers down the steeply pitched slope they had been observing from above just moments earlier. It all happened so fast. There was no time to shout or grab hold of anything, just fall. If Carlos and Rita made any sounds, they were drowned out by the roar of the wave of snow and ice now careening down the mountainous slope, cargo in tow. Sid quickly regretted removing her goggles earlier when they had started to fog, making it impossible to see where she was going. She only knew it was nowhere good.

Sid's trained instincts quickly took control of the situation. As she felt the snowy mass try to pull her down beneath the surface, she knew she had to continue to pull herself up, so pull she did. She ignored the burning in her lungs and her muscles, allowing the adrenaline that now flooded her body to force her to keep fighting.

All of a sudden she felt her breath nearly leave her when her ribcage collided with something hard, a protruding boulder most likely. The pain was immense. Stars filled her vision. She now struggled to continue swimming when all she wanted to do was clutch her right rib cage and writhe in pain.

Sid felt the ground beneath her disappear as her body fell. Into what, she did not know. She only knew that it seemed like an eternity. And then she stopped.

If it weren't for the continued sound of falling snow all around her, assaulting her senses, she might have thought she was dead. Everything she saw and felt was dark and cold. Pelted by the persistent barrage of snow and ice from above, she shut her eyes and grimaced, doing her best to prepare for what seemed an inevitable end to her story. Yet as she lay there beneath the avalanche of snow, she began to hear the roar die down, leaving space for her to now hear the groaning and moans she had apparently been uttering without realizing it.

She struggled to lift her head, propping herself up on her hands and knees. As her body painfully broke through the thin layer of snow that once separated her from the air, she gave a huge, painful gasp, sucking in air.

She was alive.

"Will! Peter! Where are you?!" she cried out frantically as hysteria threatened to break her in her already fragile state. Reality had not yet fully sunk in, but she was afraid of what her current reality might be. "Will! Peter!!" she shouted again, turning her head back and forth, trying to see anything through the pitch black darkness that surrounded her.

"Sid! It's me, I'm okay!" Will shouted to her. Relief flooded Sid's veins. He was alive, and from the sounds of it, not more than six feet away. Just as she was about to stand up and try to find him, she heard Peter shout, "Nobody move! I think we're on an ice bridge, and I don't know how wide it is!" Sid froze, almost literally. The edge could be anywhere and she wouldn't know it, so she stayed there on her hands and knees, waiting for something, anything. How much longer could she keep from breaking?

A bright light shone from behind her, illuminating their icy cage. Carefully, she sat up and rotated her neck, keeping her hands and knees safely in place, in order to see Will's headlamp shining into her eyes. "Sid! Are you okay? You look like you hurt something." Through short and ragged breaths, she managed to nod her head. Words were painful. Then another light, this time from Peter's headlamp, aided Will in illuminating the crevasse. Sid slowly took in her surroundings. The walls around them seemed to glow a dim bluish-green due to the artificial lights illuminating them. Sid quickly took note of how wide their saving grace of an ice bridge actually was. She couldn't tell if it was relief or fear she felt as her eyes measured not more than two feet from her right hand to the edge of the bridge. Two feet to the right and she would have found herself still falling until she became inevitably trapped at the bottom of the icy chasm, pinned between two walls with no hope of escape. She was lucky. They all were.

Now that Sid was starting to think more clearly, she remembered her own headlamp on her helmet and reached up to turn it on. Pain. She gritted her teeth, frustrated that even that small of an action caused her such agony. "Carlos! Rita!!" Peter shouted. Will and Sid soon joined him, as much as it pained Sid to do so. They waited in cold silence for a response but heard nothing except the hollow echo of their own desperate cries reverberating off the walls of their frozen prison. They tried several more times, waiting each time for a response from their teammates. But there was nothing. They were alone.

"Guys, check this out." Will and Sid looked in the direction where Peter's finger and head lamp pointed. "It looks like this crevasse goes on for quite a way. I don't know about you, but I don't think there's any point in us trying to climb back up the way we came down. Looks to only be about twenty feet, but the opening we fell into must be completely covered with the ice from the avalanche. That's probably why we can't see or hear anything from the outside. Even though I think we could make it to the top, there's no way we would be able to break through all of that snow, nor would we want to. I can't imagine it would take much to break through the ice and risk another wave of snow that could likely knock us off the bridge."

    "You're right," Will said, turning his gaze back down the tunnel they found themselves trapped in. "I think our best bet is to try and see if this path here leads to a section in the crevasse with an opening above. What do you guys think?" Sid looked at Peter as the two of them nodded in agreement. "Seems good to me, Will," she said. "Just so you two know, though, I think my ribcage must have hit a rock or something in the avalanche. It feels like I might have broken some ribs," she said, gingerly holding her right side. "I can still make it though, don't worry." Sid didn't want to burden either of them now of all moments. She had to be strong or they would never make it out of this mess.

(1:36 PM)

Frozen Disneyland
The three of them had been making their way through the crevasse for the past thirty minutes in relative silence with no daylight in sight. Peter and Will had placed Sid between them in case her injury caused her to trip or fall. Despite her desire to be tough and independent, Sid appreciated how these two were always watching out for her. They hadn't known each other for more than a few months and yet she already felt like

they were family. "What an incredible adventure this would have been had it not been for the fact that we might die," Sid said with an unconvincing laugh, trying to sound positive. She looked back at Will and knew he saw straight past her veil of calmness into the fear that threatened to stab her heart yet again. They continued walking.

"You know guys," Will said as the three continued to march ahead in the frozen darkness, "I could almost imagine this being some type of twisted Disneyland ride. You slide down a frozen roller coaster with a few jolts and scares, get dumped out into a giant icy pit next to a bottomless cavern of death, and then have to climb your way back up before freezing to death. Worst of all, if you can't make it up, no picture with that princess from *Frozen*!" Will's eyes and mouth opened wide in mock horror. Peter, as usual, pretended he hadn't heard Will utter such a ridiculous comment, but Will succeeded in making at least Sid chuckle, just a little. But it was enough to help her continue on.

"I've always wanted to go to Disneyland," Sid said with a silly grin plastered across her face, a grin Will shared with her, their eyes connected as if to assure the other that everything was going to be alright.

"Guys!" Peter shouted. "I think I see light up ahead!" Sid's heart skipped a beat as she strained her eyes to see past Peter. He was right! They quickly picked up their pace (the bridge had eventually filled the entire width of the crevasse, making it much safer to walk along) and hurried to their anticipated salvation. The light became brighter and brighter until they no longer required their headlamps to see where they were walking. Then they saw it: the sky. For a brief moment, the three of them stood in stunned silence, simply staring up as snowflakes drifted down and settled on their thankful faces.

Never one to waste time, Peter quickly kneeled down and began digging through his pack to assemble the gear he needed to climb the flat, icy wall before them. His would be the most difficult ascent. Since they had never planned on ice climbing, their gear for the task was limited. Peter described to them how he planned to climb. With his harness, carabiners, and ice screws, he would be forced to ascend by first inserting one screw into the ice at head height, pulling up on it in order to attach his harness to the screw, and inserting the next screw 18 inches higher than the first. Once embedded in the ice, he would unclip from the first screw in order to anchor himself to the second screw. He would then reach back down to release his first screw and begin the process all over again. It would be slow and laborious, but once he made it to the top, he would use those screws to set an anchor which he would then run their rope through, back down to Sid and Will. The two of them could ascend the rope directly by using their jumar ascenders to hoist themselves up the rope without even needing to touch the ice. "Sid, I think you should ascend before me," Will said. "That way I can take up the rear in case your ribs start causing you grief and you need someone to help push you up."

Sid subdued her pride and nodded, knowing that was probably the wisest move. As Will helped Peter gear up, Sid stopped once again to look up at the sky. No doubt Carlos and Rita had already moved on, assuming they were dead. Her eyes began to tear up at the thought of how much pain the two of them must be in right now thinking that they had lost their three friends.

"We all good?" Peter asked. Sid wiped her face quickly and nodded. It was no use worrying about such matters when they had an important task at hand: escape this icy nightmare.

"You've got this Peter," Will said, placing his hand firmly on Peter's shoulder. Peter nodded and turned toward the wall. And with that, Peter began to climb.

(2:48 PM)

Out of the Frying Pan
"I hate Disneyland," moaned Will melodramatically, rolling over into an exhausted heap away from the edge of the icy wall he had just finished ascending. Sid laughed as Peter grunted. They had made it, and through exhausted lungs and muscles, the three now collapsed on the mountainous ice field they had been trekking on a matter of hours ago. Never before had the snow- and ice-covered field they now beheld given such incredible joy and hope. Will had not yet had time to see anything but the cloudy sky above him that was steadily releasing snowflakes that drifted down and melted as they touched his warm face. His thoroughly exhausted body lay collapsed upon the snow, his chest heaving in and out as he struggled to replace the oxygen he had spent climbing out. (As he put it, "It's been a few beers since I've done something like that.")

After Sid made it to the top, fighting back tears of joy amidst tears of pain, she looked around quietly to see if there were any signs of Carlos or Rita. None.

"They think we're dead," Sid said quietly, not to anyone in particular but more to help her process what exactly was happening. She wondered if she was in shock. She could still process her surroundings, but she found it more difficult now, as if she was trying to find her way in a foggy cloud of mist.

"It appears so. Obviously there's no time to waste if we intend to catch up with them and change their minds," Peter said as he quickly slung his pack onto his two burly shoulders and began walking back in the direction they had originally come from. "Try to keep up with me, you two!" he shouted, picking up his pace.

Will and Sid looked at each other, both wary of Peter's apparent impulsive desire to go before they had even had a chance to decide as a team the best course of action.

"Peter, stop!" Will shouted at him. Peter stopped and turned around. "I get that time is of the essence right now, but don't you think we should stop and get our bearings for a second first?"

"I did get my bearings Will, right when I crawled out of that hell hole we fell into. What else is there to get? This is the way we came from, and there's no reason why the team would have gone any other direction," pointing down the eastern slope of the mountain from whence they had journeyed earlier that morning. "Come on, guys, are we taking philosophy or are we LITERALLY trying to save our lives?! We don't have time to think about the meaning of life! The only fact about life I care about right now is that the only way we can SAVE ours is by moving as fast as we can to catch up with the rest of the team. Hell, we don't even know if this was just one of numerous quakes to come, and the rest may be even worse, for all we know. By now, the guys probably have at least an hour if not more on us, so that means every minute we wait is a minute closer to getting abandoned on this damned hell hole of an island!" Sid could feel her body tensing in response to Peter's dramatic description of their current predicament. She wasn't sure if his furrowed brow and the elevated volume of his voice indicated either the strength and resolve they currently needed to survive or the foretelling of a dangerous panic that could jeopardize his ability to think clearly.

"I get it Peter, I do," Will said as he tried to reassure him. "We need to move fast, but I just think we need to take a second to maybe sit and—"

"Will, what part of 'Every minute we wait is a minute closer to getting abandoned' didn't you understand?! Look," he said as he pointed off into the distance to the path they had ascended earlier, "there's our old tracks, clear as day. Oh, wait, they're NOT clear as day anymore because every minute we waste standing around chit-chatting the more snow falls on them and covers them up!" Sid could see that stress was beginning to disrupt Peter's typically composed nature, and Will's defensive posture seemed to indicate his concurrence with her observation. As if detecting her thoughts, Peter seemed to recognize the irrationality of his hyper-sensitive emotional state. After a few deep, focused breaths, he seemed to regain a bit of his composure.

"Listen, I'm not trying to jump on you guys or be some kind of dictator. I'm really not. But I just feel that in this life or death situation, we need to approach it with some level of urgency. I mean, you guys understand, right? We just CAN'T afford to sit around if time is of the essence!"

"Peter, I get it," Sid spoke up. "Believe me, I get it. I feel the same sense of urgency. But I have to agree with Will on this. We're in a tough situation right now, but we have to choose what our most valuable asset is right now, speed or our brains, maybe both. I know it looks like the choice is clear, but if design has taught me anything, it's that the solution is seldom obvious without some hard mental groundwork."

Sid could tell by Peter's shaking head and rolling eyes that they weren't seeing eye to eye. "I appreciate your input Sid," he replied, working hard to respond with respect in spite of his tense state, "and no offense to you, but the fact of the matter is that we're not designing a pretty picture for a flower shop right now. This is REAL LIFE. It's one thing to take your time when you're designing stuff or whatever, but right now we don't have that luxury. This is the kind of situation where you've got to just respond. That's what saves lives on the battlefield. That's what's going to get us back to the boat. That is the ONLY thing that will save us!"

The next few minutes were filled with all three intensely trying to explain to the others their reasoning. While Will mostly agreed with Sid's proposal to wait and think through their situation, she was wary of the fact that he was nearly just as eager to *vamanos* and move quickly back to the boat. The debate was heavy, and each person had a certain level of reasoning behind their proposed choice of action. Despite their best attempts to get the others to see their sides, in the end, Peter could not be persuaded to wait any longer. They all knew that they had intended to stick together, but Will proposed that since agreement was clearly impossible, perhaps their taking different strategies might actually increase their odds of finding the group. Then, whoever found the group first could signal the other two with the flares they had left aboard the ship. Sid's inner wisdom all but screamed that it was a terrible idea, but she knew resistance was futile at this point.

"Alright Peter," she said quietly, already regretting what she was about to say. "You know I don't like this idea of us separating, but if you really won't wait any longer, I guess all we can do is hope one of us finds the team and we can help finish the reunion with the others." Scarcely had those words escaped her mouth when Peter resolutely nodded his head and set off in a dead sprint down the descending snow field. She turned her eyes away to keep Will from seeing how Peter's actions, and even more so his snide remark about her profession, had hurt her.

"I don't just draw pretty pictures," she muttered under her breath.

(3:15 PM)

Chapter 2

THE STRUGGLE IS REAL

"What's certain is that the world is changing faster than at any time in human history."
— Philip Stevens

(4:58 PM)

What was it Peter had felt slowly grabbing at his chest more and more over the past twenty minutes? Exhaustion? Perhaps. He had, after all, been descending across the ice field at roughly four miles an hour without stopping for so much as a water break, and all with the intimate companionship of his thirty pounds of gear and victuals in his rucksack.

But I've felt physical exhaustion before, and this is something more, he thought, his body expertly moving in a coordinated rhythm: three steps forward as he forced the cold air in through his frozen nostrils, three more as he forced the CO_2 out through his mouth, each breath fortified with purpose and control. It was this disciplined breathing pattern that had helped him finish (and get close to winning a couple of times) numerous long-distance races, including his town's local marathon just a couple of months ago. He was glad he had traded his glasses for contacts today because the warm air his mouth was pumping out would have instantly turned to annoying moisture upon the cold lenses, and hindrances like that were unacceptable.

Hindrances...

That must be the gnawing feeling inside my chest, he decided, a mere mental hindrance, and one that must be overcome through endurance and equal amounts of mental and physical fortitude. Otherwise, it would relentlessly force him to question the wisdom of his actions. But he couldn't resist the questions that were barraging his mind like an army besieging a castle gate with battering rams amidst the deafening war cries of the attacking army, hell bent on breaking down every last defense of that city.

What if Will and Sydney were right and I should have just waited a little longer to think about the situation? The resolution he had enjoyed when he first started out on his return trek, now almost a half hour ago, was all but vacant, replaced instead with near crippling uncertainty that was now threatening to block what little oxygen he was able to breathe into his weary and exhausted lungs.

"Get a grip, Peter," he muttered to himself through ragged breaths with disgust, trying desperately once again to clear his mind and focus on the task at hand.

Thud!

"Sh*t!" Peter yelled through pain and gritted teeth as his body was propelled downward onto the ice. Tenderly, he grabbed at his throbbing left shin. He wasn't even sure what it was exactly that had so violently connected with his leg, probably just a well-camouflaged chunk of ice. Whatever it was had tripped him enough to make him fall helplessly through the air with only the icy ground to absorb his fall.

"You idiot!" he angrily yelled to himself, grimacing

through the pain as he slowly picked himself back up from the ground. He chastised himself for such costly ignorance, adjusted his belt strap, and took the opportunity for a much needed drink of water, which only became available after much twisting of his now frozen tube that fed into the large water bladder in his pack. After he sipped the deliciously cool, refreshing water, he also took the opportunity to survey his surroundings as he painfully tried to walk off his avoidable injury. He peered across the ice in all directions and failed to spot even one footprint. He did, however, detect something else: rocks. Despite all the pain that now plagued his leg (not to mention that the rest of his body wasn't exactly feeling like he had just returned from the spa), Peter could once again feel a source of hope welling up inside him. He felt as if he was running a 100-yard touchdown and had just crossed the 10-yard line! If he remembered correctly, their trek from the beach where they had anchored and set up camp to the start of the ice field had been probably no more than four to five miles, and the place where they had fallen into the crevasse had most likely been a similar distance from the beginning of the ice field. *Okay, so maybe the 50-yard line*, Peter thought as he did his math one more time.

    He was confused. He knew beyond a shadow of a doubt that he had traveled at a minimum five to six miles, though he suspected it was closer to seven. Now that he thought about it, Peter realized he should have started to reevaluate his azimuth a couple of miles ago when he had failed to reach the boulder field. But here he was, just a stone's throw from the boundary, and he was more than happy to overlook the mathematical incongruence now that he felt that much closer to his group.

    "HEY! CARLOS! RITA!! HEEEEEYYYY!" After waiting

in silent expectation for several seconds, he reasoned that there was still plenty of trees and terrain between him and their probable location, which likely kept them from being able to hear his shouts.

  He felt refreshed again, both physically and mentally. With a new spring in his step (a real feat with a now throbbing shin), he continued down the steep slope, this time minding his step as he maneuvered around the occasional boulder peaking its crusty head through the icy surface. Travel was much faster once he reached the rock field because he was more confident in his steps. Skipping from rock to rock, as if weightless, Peter felt so free. Something about being surrounded by the wild unexplored terrain mixed with the physical and mental challenge that lay before him made him feel more alive than he'd ever felt before. Back home, he was an avid hiker and knew every single trail around him like the back of his hand. Granted, there wasn't more than a 500-foot change in elevation for miles around him and the available hiking trails were pretty slim, but what was there he knew better than anyone! He pushed himself up yet another hill in the now mostly flat terrain, his legs and lungs on fire from the rapid pace he had set for himself. He gasped with delight as he saw the tree line that had previously been hidden from sight. *Only a couple more miles to go!* Now it felt like he was finally at that 10-yard line.

  As he entered into the lush and humid rainforest (not before quickly stopping to shed some layers into his pack), rocks were replaced with moist, dark soil and ice with tall, verdant trees. Instead of ice chunks, the only thing blocking his way now was the vegetation that sought to entangle him as he sprinted through the jungle. The chorus of wildlife around him became a stadium full of cheering fans, fanatically spurring on their team's star receiver to victory! Even though his legs and lungs still burned, it seemed like nothing now that he knew he must be getting closer. Amidst his bright and joyful thoughts of discovering his teammates again and how thrilled they would be to hear how swiftly he had acted in order to reconnect with them, there was but one thought that nagged at the back of his mind: nothing seemed familiar. Perhaps the sun beginning to set on him was making the landscape a bit harder to navigate. He had also been so focused on reaching the summit yesterday and today that, to be honest, he hadn't spent much time marking his location or remembering significant landmarks. *Well, no matter*. Once he reached the shoreline, it would be a piece of cake to walk along the shore until he found the ship and, hence, his teammates.

So onward he sped. The downward slope of his return trip made the going much faster. He liked going fast. It made him feel like he was once again back home in an endurance trail race, only this time the stakes were much higher. This thought kept him going, one stride after the other, as he pushed branches out of his way and leaped over a stray fallen log or two.

The thinker loses to the doer, he thought, congratulating himself (with as much modesty as he could muster) for his action-oriented approach to solving problems. He wasn't one to brag, but he did enjoy knowing that his strengths were useful.

Peter suddenly slowed his pace, just for a second. He could scarcely believe it. There, twenty yards in front of him shone the light through the trees, meaning the edge of the forest was close at hand. With his heart pounding fast within his chest, lungs heaving in and out, and sweat dripping from his hot and furrowed brow, he slowed down to stop and listen. It took him a while to hear anything except the sound of utter exhaustion desperately escaping from his dry, cracked lips, but then he heard something else: ocean waves.

Peter swore to himself then and there that he would never forget this moment, not for the rest of his days. There it was at last, the end zone. Peter half jogged, half stumbled through the remaining bit of forest between him and his point of rescue, his sweet relief from the hellish nightmare he had been forced into. He brushed the back of his hand across his lips to wipe away the frothy saliva at the corners of his exhausted and droopy mouth and began to see bigger and bigger sections of the golden sunset as he got closer and closer to the edge. Peter was sure he must look like a small child on Christmas morning, but he couldn't care less. He coaxed his arms and legs to keep pumping, to cross the finish line, to score the touchdown. He started announcing his presence again at the top of his voice, yelling with everything that was within him (he was too tired to care that his words were completely incoherent), hoping that he wasn't too late. And as he finally burst beyond the final tree onto the pebble-strewn beach, his eyes fixated on the ocean that now lay—

Peter froze. Something wasn't right.

Looking from left to right, trying to get his bearings, he struggled to find any of the landmarks from their campsite the past few nights, like the jagged 100-foot embankment he clearly recalled wrapping around from just up the hill from their campsite out into the water, forming the outer perimeter that had made their little sandy cove such an ideal location to set anchor, protected from the elements.

Sandy cove...

Peter looked down at his muddy boots, thoroughly soaked by now, and slowly dug his feet into the pebbles underneath them.

They were pebbles, not sand.

He racked his brain trying to reason through this strange scene that now lay before his eyes, the vast, uninterrupted views of the ocean, turning more and more crimson each minute from the sun that was slowly setting off to his left. But how could his views be uninterrupted?

And most importantly, why was the sun on his left?

The cove they had anchored in lay on the island's southeastern shore, which would mean the sunset would be on his right. It was all too much to take in. Peter didn't want to believe it but as he sank to his knees, he realized that instead of escaping his nightmare, it had just gotten worse.

Peter had mistakenly arrived on the island's northeast shore, the exact opposite of where he needed to be.

(5:35 PM)

(3:21 PM)

Cold Regret
She looks so calm, Will thought, looking at Sid in admiration. She was just ten yards away, perched on one of the large boulders of ice that populated the ice field, sitting cross legged with a sketch book and pen in her hands, but her determined gaze could have been focusing on something ten light years away. Will could see the calm focus in her eyes, as if they were seeing something that no one else could. He turned toward the direction she was looking, half to see if he could see what it was she was fixated on, half to simply move his body and warm his cold limbs and digits. The temperature couldn't be much lower than 20 degrees Fahrenheit, but with the consistent movement of air flowing from the top of the bowl that lay above them, it certainly felt 20 degrees colder than that.

As he rubbed his shoulders with his thick gloves and shuffled his boots around to keep his blood moving, it reminded him of the frustrating fact that they themselves were not moving. They had only just lost sight of Peter a few minutes ago as he sprinted off down the hill, the gray mist now completely encompassing his bright red coat that Will had gotten so used to seeing in front of him throughout their journey. He regretted not having been able to figure out a reasonable solution that all three of them could agree to. It's true that their nerves were definitely frayed from the adrenaline overdose their bodies had just endured in the past couple of hours. This was also the first time any of them had been forced to make any major decisions the entire trip. Without Carlos around to call the shots, they had found themselves plagued with indecision over what to do next.

Before Peter had left, the conversation had quickly escalated, leaving Will feeling now slightly foolish at how his typically calm and composed nature had been so quickly undone by the pressure. It certainly wasn't out of anger toward Peter by any means. Ever since meeting Peter just six months ago, he had developed a deep respect for the man and his charismatic strength. He was the type of man who always had a plan and was always willing to initiate it, like the friend who broke the never-ending banter about what movie to watch and just picked a freakin' movie. This strength had served as a powerful advantage throughout their trip, ensuring that all of the essential tasks got done. Peter had shown himself to be quite the handyman, never seeming to encounter an obstacle he hadn't dealt with before.

That's not to say that Peter's "confidence" in his abilities were always appreciated. There had been a handful of times when Peter's self-proclaimed omniscience caused the group tension, particularly with Sid. Each time, Peter had insisted to some member of the team that his or her method for achieving the task at hand was inadequate, to which he would proceed by instructing them on how he had always done it (the correct way, that is). While it seemed to amuse most of the team, not least of whom was Carlos, it flustered Sid to no end, much to Will's bemusement. The team had quickly learned it was best to leave her alone for a bit after one of her and Peter's "episodes." They knew that after a brief period of brooding and a few powerfully composed sketches in her sketchbook, Sidney would settle down again, and the two would apologize. Then, shortly after, the team spirit would always kick back in full gear. Will chuckled as he recalled one such disagreement when he happened to oversee her sketching a frantic figure (no doubt Peter) being chased down by a herd of some frightening wildebeests or some other fantastical creature.

But now Peter was gone.

The two had wasted no time after Peter left, again trying to decide how they were going to reach the boat and their team. "Since Peter has decided to try to catch the rest of the group by following our tracks—even though I think his decision was impulsive and not well thought out—maybe we can try to use that to our advantage," Sydney said with that same spark Will saw in her eyes every time a situation or challenge called upon her ingenuity and creativity. "It's killing me that I haven't thought of something that I feel will work yet, but I'm sure we can come up with something if we both put our heads together."

Will laughed quietly under his breath as he thought about the irony of how rapidly the words she spoke about not moving too quickly shot out of her mouth, reminding him of their very first encounter all those months ago. She had been quick to tell him she was a graphic designer shortly after their introduction during their first team rendezvous. "Not the kind that just makes cute birthday cards but like a legit marketing graphic designer," she had clarified. Out of sheer courtesy, he had responded by asking her what it was that drew her to that career.

That's when he first saw the spark, an omen of the verbal onslaught he was now powerless to avoid.

By the time he realized he had just opened Pandora's box of Sydney's passion for design, it was too late. Despite the multiple desperate glances toward his teammates, all of which were returned by sadistically humorous grins and Carlos's mouthing the words "good luck," Will found himself helpless to escape the enthusiastic logorrhea Sydney began to pour out upon his unsuspecting ears. Amongst many topics, she described to him in great length why Papyrus was the greatest travesty to have ever been inflicted upon typography (closely followed by Comic Sans), how beveled font should be outlawed from humanity ("1996 called; they want their font back," as she put it), and the horrors of working with clients who insisted on printing 30 kB .jpeg pictures at 18" wide.

 He had all but diverted his attention to the significantly more interesting piece of down feather hanging from the left side of her hair—what held it to her hair despite the merciless whiplashing it received from her excited shakings and body expressions was beyond his human understanding—when a change of tone sucked him back into their "conversation." She began to share with him (in as somber of a tone as one would expect in discussing topics such as existentialism, self-determination, or one's dog dying) the nearly untapped potential she perceived of design in the world.

 Thinking back on that moment, Will remembered how her description of design's unique ability to transform the world for good had captured his mind, quickly shifting his eyes from her friendly face feather to her eyes, eyes that seemed so...so distant...no, not distant, but rather...focused. It was as if that wild spark had been transfigured from a tiny ember into something not quite of this world, something heavenly. It was the same focus she had now, what appeared an almost trancelike state. In his mind, he imagined she was paying homage to the goddess of design, silently pleading for but a silent word in response to their holy prayer for guidance in their current plight, a tiny request in return for her undivided worship.

 As he stood there, allured by her nearly transcendental state, he couldn't help but feel a part of him deep inside that desired that same ability to harness his own creativity. It was a power he had always envied in others but had never quite been able to wield himself. Yet just before he was sure he would lose himself to the holy abyss his mind now teetered on, an icy voice whispered into his ear, "But there's no time…" and he was once again jolted back to reality, the reality that seconds were transforming into minutes, and with each minute came an increased sense of urgency to act.

 Before it was too late.

No Time

Will was no rookie when it came to games of strategy like the one he was playing now. As an accountant for a medium-sized construction firm in his home town, he had spent the past fifteen years harnessing his innate eye for details. Every task he took on he would approach with a thorough yet efficient method of attack, knowing that one reckless move could cost his company thousands of dollars in one way or another. Only once had he made that mistake in his younger years, and he swore to himself he would never do that again.

 Since that costly life lesson, Will had built a reputation amongst his colleagues as being both responsible as well as approachable, so much so that they had fondly bestowed upon him the nickname "Flush" due to his ability to "always deal with everyone else's crap." (He vowed his teammates would never discover this potentially socially fatal nickname). Though he was humble enough not to flaunt it, Will knew it was unlikely that there was a challenge within his job that he had not already faced before and figured out. That's why he had directed his competitive nature toward improving the speed and efficiency with which he completed his work.

Whether it was financial record organization systems, cost reduction strategies, or searching for maximum deductions, Will knew his field inside and out.

Now, instead of listening to the sound of numbers crunching in his head, his ears could only hear the sound of snow crunching underneath his restless boots pacing back and forth, back and forth, as he worked furiously to wrap his logical brain around what outcome Sid could possibly be searching for that wasn't already blatantly obvious. Half out of humor, half out of frustration, he quietly muttered to himself, "We're all going to die."

"What's that?" Sydney asked. *So, she's not completely lost in space*, Will thought sarcastically. "I said 'Just take your time!'"

Dang it. That was the last thing he wanted to tell her! As he looked down at his watch, he was horrified to discover it had now been twenty minutes since Peter had left. Twenty minutes of wasted time spent reinventing the wheel, yet here they were now without so much as a snowball to account for their efforts. Just an empty snow field now hardened by boot prints Will had repeatedly stamped upon it through his pacing.

Finally, Will knew that he could wait no longer. With or without Sid, he knew he had to find a way to rescue him and his teammates. "Sid, listen, we need to get going now or Peter will be right and we won't make it back to the team in time. It's time to move." There was no doubt in his mind that now was the time for action, not meditation.

"I know Will, believe me, I know we need to move! It's just that there's something gnawing at the back of my brain telling me there's a better way, and it's right in front of us! I understand that every minute is precious, which is why I'm trying so hard to think of ALL the possibilities we have! If you just give me another few minutes I'm sure—"

"Sid, that's what you said the past three times that I've told you we need to start going!" Will racked his brain trying desperately to reach through to the sense of reason he was sure she possessed. "We both know that it won't take Carlos and the others more than a half hour to load up all the gear back into the boat and head out. We've already lost more than an hour, and we just can't afford to lose any more!" Will was desperate to convince her but he could see in Sid's eyes that she was determined to create a better wheel.

"Listen, I know that Peter was hasty, and believe me, I'm praying that his haste doesn't get him lost or worse. But if we keep our eyes up and don't take any more than the absolute minimum number of breaks, we can still make it back to the beach before they leave! But you have to trust me when I say we need to leave NOW, or better yet five minutes ago. Please Sid, I don't want to leave you here by yourself."

He suspected before that he would be unable to convince her of his logic but—there it was again, that spark in her eye—and then he knew it. There was no changing her mind. "Will, you've got to do what you think is right. Honestly, this just sucks without Carlos here to just boss us around." Will nodded and smiled ever so slightly, but it did little to change the situation. "I'm sure that Jon Krakauer would tell us that splitting up is only good for story plots where everyone dies, but I'm afraid I just need to stick to my gut on this one. I'm sorry but I just KNOW that there's a better solution. I just need to give myself the time and space to snatch it out of the air. Will you trust me?"

"Sid, I trust that you're only doing this because you think it's the best choice, but like you said, I've got to do what I think is right. And I'm afraid that if neither of us get going and Peter gets himself lost in the jungle, which is unfortunately very likely, we will miss our chance for good. I promise though that as soon as I find the group, I'll come back for you. If you do end up leaving, be sure to mark your trail with marking tape wherever you go, and I'll do the same, okay? That way you can find me if you change your mind and I can find you when I meet up with the rest of the team."

  Sid nodded in agreement. Will didn't like it any more than she did, but if he was going to save them, he knew he had to act. They both walked toward each other to embrace like they had done so many other times on their trip. With all they had been through, Sid felt more like a sister to him than a comrade he had only known for a few short months.

  And with that, they said their goodbyes. If it had been anyone but Sid, Will would have felt nervous about leaving someone behind. But she had shown him and the rest of the group time and time again that she was more than capable of taking care of herself.

  Will turned and walked back to where he had laid down his pack and brushed off the light layer of snow that had accumulated since he set it down almost a half hour ago. Picking it up by the strap and placing it back on his shoulders, he adjusted the straps one last time and set off.

(3:34 PM)

(4:20 PM)

The Dragon's Tail
"I remember you, rock!" Will had to admit one of the joys of traveling alone was the freedom to speak to in-

animate objects free of judgement from those self-righteous parents as they slowly pulled their children away from the guy talking to himself. He grinned as he leaned against the large familiar boulder behind him while he gingerly sipped at his now nearly half-empty water bladder, his chest heaving in and out as he tried to catch his breath. He was grinning because he remembered how close this boulder was to the dirt trail they had blazed earlier that morning, which meant he was getting close to the tiny cove they had anchored in.

    Which meant he was getting close to finding his teammates.

    For forty-five minutes or so he had managed to keep a strong pace (though he was careful not to push too hard, seeing as he had just wreaked havoc on his lungs from his unexpected ice climb). True to his meticulous accounting nature, Will had also made sure not to become too engrossed in efficiency to lose precious precision. He kept the fresh hand-drawn map of the island he and Sid had put together zipped safely in his chest pocket where it would be easy to access. His plan was quite simple. Just like he had climbed the trees earlier in order to gain their bearing as they were making their way toward the mountain, he planned to do likewise once he got back to the trees and into the densely overgrown foliage. It had been simple enough to follow their tracks across the snow field. Once he reached the scree slope, however, he planned on setting his azimuth due east and slightly south, picking one land marker at a time and being sure to continually look up to ensure he was on track. He was surprised how often he found himself veering ever so slightly off course. As he had descended down the rocky slope, keeping his eyes on the small outcrop of trees within the field that he had remembered passing on the way up, his mind was already thinking ahead to the next landmark he could use to keep himself heading in the right direction.

Reaching into his pack that now lay on the ground beside him while he rested, he pulled out an energy bar and began to slowly chew on it as he again took stock of his surroundings. While he was almost positive he was still on course, he had expected to see some sign of the cove by now. *I suppose everyone always thinks they've gone farther than they actually have when they're tired*, he thought, racking his brain trying to remember what lay over that rock-covered slope that now blocked his view while simultaneously trying to remember why in God's good earth he had picked carrot cake-flavored bars instead of oatmeal raisin walnut.

"Nobody's perfect," he said to the remaining bite in his hand before finishing it off with a grimace. After a much-needed palette cleanse from his water, he again suited up, took a deep breath, and began to ascend the slope that lay before him. For a brief second, he almost bid his rocky companion farewell before deciding against it. Best not to engrain bad social habits.

As he approached the peak of the small hill, he raised his head up…and beamed. There it was, beyond the green blanket of trees that now lay at his feet. That large section of rock that formed a semi-circle around their boat, with its tall, jagged ridge line, was now barely perceptible through the scattered cluster of clouds in the sky. From where he stood, he smiled as he imagined it to be a dragon's tail, gently folded across the salty water while the vast array of trees that made up its wings and body lay still and silent, as if waiting to be awakened. Will quickly began to descend down toward his salvation. He made it easily to the tree line and kept his compass handy in order to verify that he was still on track. Every once in a while, he would be stopped by an obstacle such as a creek or a large protrusion of unscalable granite, where he would be forced to temporarily stray off course. However, once his path was again unobstructed, he would climb one of the taller yet manageable trees he could find, just enough so that he could break through the veiling crown of leaves and branches that inhibited his view from below, locate the top of the rock's ridge line once again, reset his declination, and then descend once more.

  He continued this process as he progressed through the jungle. He knew not to be alarmed at the differences he found in his environment from his journey the day before, as he was on a different but still correct path toward the cove. So long as he kept those cliffs within his sights, or at least stayed true to his calculated declination, he knew he would eventually end up back at the beach.

(4:55 PM)

(5:19 PM)

Gone With the Wind

Will stopped. What was that he heard? It could have just been the leaves rustling in the wind, he supposed. He picked up his pace as he worked his way even faster through the forest. The noise was louder now, and he began to follow it. Soon, his eyes saw what his ears had whispered before: the river. Upon this new discovery, Will quickly began to gather his thoughts. He remembered there being an estuary that opened out into the ocean just south of where they had set up camp (that was where they had gotten their fresh water). Based upon his projected proximity to the beach (he estimated he was no more than three quarters of a mile away from the shore based upon his most recent tree climbing escapade), he reasoned that it was very unlikely that there were any other major bodies of water within such close proximity to each other given the large current flow in this river. Therefore, he figured that if he simply followed the river, it would of course take him to his destination: the beach!

    Will quickly began to follow the meandering stream to its logical point of termination, straying only occasionally and for a short distance whenever strict adherence to its edge proved to be too difficult and inefficient to navigate. Once or twice he nearly slipped into the river when trying to move too quickly due to his haste, and he chastised himself, forcing himself to gain his composure and once again continue on at a healthy and reasonable pace.

    After twenty minutes or so of following the river and its snaking progress through the dense jungle, Will saw what his eyes had been searching for. Indeed, the light through the trees began to grow more and more prominent. Now he knew he was close, and this thought was confirmed as he began to hear the crashing of the waves and smell the salt air of the ocean, getting closer every step!

    Will's thoughts turned to his comrades as he quickened his pace, leaping over fallen trees and ducking under low hanging branches. He thought about how happy they would be when they saw him and found out that Sid and Peter were also alive. "Carlos will definitely cry," he smirked. Carlos tried to come across as a real tough guy, "but he's just a big gooey gummy bear," Will said to himself. With all luck, Peter had already given the team the news, and all that would be left would be to find Sid and get home. With his face beaming, he crashed beyond the final row of trees and ran out onto the beautiful white sandy beach, the beach where he could finally rest knowing he was safe. He had made it! Yes, there was the tall tail of a protrusion of rocks that had so graciously beckoned him back, curving gracefully inlet as they traversed out into the salty water. He was on the opposite side of the estuary from where the boat was docked, but as he began to look back into the jungle to try to find a good place to cross over, he paused.

The boat. Where was it?

He looked back out to the south where the boat had been just that morning, but all he saw was the same virgin beauty they had seen when they first arrived here days ago. He strained his eyes across the beach to find where they had set up camp, but now he saw nothing but the empty canvas of sandy beach they had first witnessed as they pulled into the bay, save for the addition of several sets of human footprints. *Maybe I'm misremembering where we set up base*, Will thought, and he frantically set off back into the jungle to find a place to cross the river so that he could adequately get his bearings and figure out whether he was going crazy or if he was simply...no, he couldn't say it.

After a couple of minutes of backtracking, Will found a set of protruding, though slightly slippery, rocks within the river and cautiously crossed to the other side. Returning back to the beach now, his mind and heart raced with the sinking fear that he was right, that he had not made it in time, and that he had missed his one chance of escape. As he again broke through the tree line, this time now almost exactly where he remembered they had entered the jungle yesterday, he shook his head in numb, disbelief: the beach was empty. He walked over to the place in the sand where the team had pitched their tents, peering into the small fireplace they had sat around just the other night, discussing with excitement what might lie ahead of them, what they may find on their journey to summit the mountain. No one could have predicted what would have happened next.

As reality set in, he half sat, half fell to the ground, too shocked to know what else he could do. What else could he do? The team had left, probably in a hurry in order to get back to safety. Or perhaps it had been out of grief from losing their teammates. Regardless, the only thing that connected them now was the wind at their backs, propelling one toward home and the other toward despair.

He was too late.

(5:33 PM)

CASE STUDY
with Will Haughey

COMPANY TYPE	Private
YEAR FOUNDED	2006
LOCATION	Darien, CT
ESTIMATED REVENUE	$5 million
APPROXIMATE NUMBER OF EMPLOYEES	25[1]

Impact

Have you ever wondered where your children's toys come from? If you're like me, then the answer is (unfortunately) no. However, if you're anything like brothers Will and Chris Haughey, you not only ask the question, you help forge a new answer. Tegu is a toy company that specializes in simple yet beautiful magnetic wooden blocks, but the impact goes beyond mere blocks and is incredibly powerful in our discussion of innovation in social impact design.

You might say it is even "magnetic."

While speaking at an entrepreneurship conference known as Praxis, Will Haughey explained Tegu's mission is "to change the way your kids play and create social change in one of the poorest nations in the Western Hemisphere." At the very heart of the toy enterprise is a desire to orchestrate social equity in Honduras by creating fair wage, equitable jobs within the country as

[1]"Tegu's Competitors"

opposed to exporting those jobs elsewhere. Tegu is also committed to improving the lives of the children in the community in which they work. Hundreds of children in Tegucigalpa, Honduras, are unable to attend school and are instead forced to scavenge for their livelihood in the city's trash collection. That's why Tegu committed to partnering with a local school called Amor, Fe y Esperanza (Love, Faith and Hope) that helps children escape poverty by providing them an opportunity to receive an education.

While the wood for their products was originally sourced directly out of Honduras, Tegu currently obtains its raw building material from sustainably harvested shade trees on coffee plantations in Guatemala. This business relationship with Guatemalan coffee plantations has not only proved itself to be profitable for Tegu (by paying 30 percent lower than global market prices), but it's also increasing revenue for the plantations by providing an alternative revenue stream outside of their direct product and selling lower grades of wood that are often considered waste due to their lower desirability (as Tegu products are able to utilize smaller, less usable pieces of wood). "It's good for us because the price is right and it's good for them because they're using up inventory," says Will. "Our primary focus is job creation. Our core mission is about people, specifically creating opportunities for people through profit."

While social equity is at the forefront of Tegu's existence, they also recognize the vital role a healthy ecosystem plays in the lives of all Hondurans. This inspired Tegu to sustainably harvest their tree stock, which includes planting up to 6,000 saplings for every tree they harvest. Tegu so firmly stands behind these two values of equitable jobs and environmental sustainability that they've printed it on their product boxes: "Social impact through jobs and responsible sourcing."

Story
When I met Will in the summer of 2017, I was more than impressed with his story and his extensive success, and apparently success runs in the family. Before co-founding Tegu, Will's older brother Chris received his bachelor's in mechanical engineering from Stanford in 2002 while Will received his bachelor's in business administration from Indiana University in 2004.

It's evident that Chris has long had an interest in Central and South America. After graduation, he spent a year in Mexico working with university students, then continued his work in Latin America after joining the Boston Consulting Group, where he spent a good amount of time traveling. While on a business trip in Honduras, Chris experienced firsthand the extreme poverty in the South American nation. Having a knack for business, Chris saw more than just a charitable need; he saw an opportunity to "address poverty in a more sustainable way by harnessing business."

He and his brother Will began conducting market research and validation for a year, searching for what product Honduras could offer the world. They discovered the country's rich supply of hardwood trees and learned of recently concerted efforts to improve the sustainability of the way in which they were harvested. At that same time, the brothers became fascinated with the elegant yet timeless beauty of European wooden toy blocks. In an effort to "bring the toys into the 21st century," they reinvented the wooden block by embedding powerful magnets within the blocks, making a simple yet fascinating tool for children to unlock their imagination, all without instructions or on/off switches. Chris launched Tegu in the spring of 2007. Meanwhile, Will had been experiencing great success in the investment banking world at Goldman Sachs after his graduation. In 2008, Will joined his brother at Tegu full time.

Innovation
In spite of Tegu's deep passion for providing equitable and fair wages for work in impoverished countries such as Honduras, the brothers realized that good intentions rarely create real results. For this reason, they chose to design their business model around the idea that profit can be used to power a sustainable force for social impact: "Our primary focus is job creation. Our core mission is about people, specifically creating opportunities for people through profit." Many might say that job creation isn't very "social impactish," but try telling that to the Honduran men and women without good jobs who need to provide a livelihood for their families. Tegu's mission of job creation and sustainable product sourcing could be the very key to help local communities pull themselves up out of poverty into more secure and equitable conditions.

Very few for-profit companies are explicitly connected to actively promoting social impact. Even fewer have integrated their specific social impact pursuit within the heart of their business model. Tegu stands as a powerful example of a successful company in a unique product market not typically associated with strong social impact, and it has done so by placing great care and thought not only into their high quality product but also in the "design before the design," in the very essence of how they meet their "double bottom line"* (more in Chapter 7) of social impact through sustainable profit.

Whether for good or other, since so many companies out there have gotten on the "cause-based marketing" bandwagon, Will says it is no longer an option to create appeal based solely on the recipient of that organization's charity. Many will point to the formation of Toms Shoes as the catalyst of the recent surge in cause-based marketing. "Very rarely is that social good so universally appealing that it creates differentiation for your products," says Will, explaining that "the business is the impact."

Advice
- **Don't Rely on the Cause**
    o Toms Shoes stands as a testament to the power of cause-based marketing and how it can skyrocket the popularity of a product. However, whether for good or otherwise, Will states that there are now so many cause-based marketing companies that it is no longer viable to depend heavily on your cause to create demand for your product: "Very rarely is that social good so universally appealing that it creates differentiation for your products."

Chapter 3

INNOVATE OR DIE

"Risk is the will to act on imagination."
- Beth Comstock

In Chapter 2, both Peter and Will showed us the dangers of failing to innovate solutions. In Peter's case, his decision to move before adequately considering the correct form of action, combined with his lack of awareness that he was straying off course, ultimately sabotaged his efforts to reconnect with his teammates. While Will paid more attention to his surroundings, and hence remained on course, his single-mindedness in choosing a course of action also prohibited him from finding Carlos and Rita. He ended up where he *thought* he wanted to be; he just didn't know that rescue lay elsewhere.

While diligence and hard work are essential to progress and success, the inability to observe opportunities and learn from past mistakes will severely handicap any attempt to pursue relevance in today's day and age. In this chapter, we will explore more specifically the threats to organizations that either don't innovate or don't do it well.

Three Tragedies

In 1985, an innovative new entertainment franchise called Blockbuster was born (kids born after 2004, ask your parents). Twenty percent of Americans now owned VCRs as opposed to just half of that the previous year, so the fields were ripe for the harvest. As with many great innovations, Blockbuster's initial success can largely be attributed to founder David Cook's attention to the screaming opportunity of an exploding number of home movie watchers. By 1992, Blockbuster was indisputably leading the video rental industry, boasting over 2,800 stores worldwide. In 2004, Blockbuster reached the pinnacle of its market dominance, as evidenced by their 9,000 stores globally. It appeared they had the stake on the market.[1] Yet just a few years earlier, in 1997, a Silicon Valley veteran, frustrated at Blockbuster after being charged $40 in late fees, founded a new company that would come to be Blockbuster's undoing.[2] It would take time for this corporate overthrow to take place.

This new second-string company started with the revolutionary idea of not selling movie rentals but rather subscriptions to both limited and unlimited rentals. Once a customer picked a subscription, he or she could then select online any movie they wanted to watch, and the movie would then be shipped directly to their door. While this new model of service was a bit timelier and certainly less conducive to spontaneity in selecting entertainment, one of the benefits that solidified the beginning of their market dominance was the absence of late fees. Having purchased a recurring subscription, one could simply keep the movie as long as they wanted with no fear of annoying $40 late fees, thus satisfying both the customer with the freedom to watch the mov-

---

[1] Company Man. "The Decline of Blockbuster."
[2] Phillips and Ferdman. "A Brief, Illustrated History."

ie whenever they pleased and the company with the continual cash influx of subscription fees. However, it wasn't until 2004 that the underdog would come to steal the show in movie entertainment with the creation of its online video on demand service.[3]

By now, you've probably guessed that this company is Netflix. Netflix claims to be "the world's leading internet entertainment service with over 139 million paid members in over 190 countries enjoying TV series, documentaries and features films across a wide variety of genres and languages."[4] In 2010, Blockbuster was left dazed in the luminous aftermath of Netflix's triumphal victory, forced to declare bankruptcy in order to pay back $1 billion in debt. The company struggled to survive over the coming three years, being sold to DISH Network for a measly $234 million in cash in 2011. In 2013, it officially announced plans to close its remaining US stores.[5]

It is interesting to note that Blockbuster's demise was not due to their refusal to innovate but rather their delayed response in doing so. Blockbuster knew that Netflix was on to something critical, yet they were unable to act in time to meet the demands of the changing culture. After all, Blockbuster had built an entire empire upon a compensation system dependent upon late fees. To have changed this would have required massive amounts of infrastructure adaptation. They say it's easier to turn a small tug boat than a large barge, and Blockbuster was certainly no tug boat.

Let's jump back in time to 1899 in Detroit, Michigan. Beginning with just $8,000 and two stores, Sebastian S.

---

3 Phillips and Ferdman
4 "Netflix." Netflix Investors.
5 Phillips and Ferdman

Kresge and his partner Charles J. Wilson started the S. S. Kresge Company. After years of growth and numerous acquisitions, S. S. Kresge would open the very first Kmart in Garden City, Michigan. Kmart's success grew over time, gaining the reputation as the store with the most affordable products. In the 90s, they would become the number two retail store in America, surpassed only by the behemoth known as Walmart. In 1992, the company would go on to purchase Borders Bookstore (an ominously prophetic relationship due to Border's eventual foreclosure), adding to its previous purchases of Sports Authority and OfficeMax in 1992.[6]

However, by 1995, the company had sold most of these corporate investments due to decreased business, and its decline was only to continue. In 2002, Kmart was forced to file for bankruptcy while still gasping for breath. Between the years 2006 and 2016, store locations decreased from 1,388 to 735, and revenue followed in a similar trajectory.[7] The company's net income has been negative since 2011, leading many to wonder how it has even managed to survive at all.

What exactly was Kmart's Achilles heel that doomed it for certain destruction? Most agree that the company's pivotal mistake was its refusal or inability to innovate. *Forbes* contributor Kern Lewis writes this:

> While Kmart settled into a comfortable pattern of expansion, its leaders failed to properly manage the brand to keep up with the competition. Its rivals, Wal-Mart[8] in particular, upped the ante by offering great prices and great service. Kmart

---

[6] Company Man. "The Decline of Kmart."
[7] Company Man. "The Decline of Kmart."
[8] Doug McMillon, President and CEO of Walmart, announced on December 6, 2017, that they are changing the company's name from Wal-Mart to Walmart, effective February 1, 2018.

never responded to this shift, continuing to deliver a sub-par customer service experience.[9]

The fact that Kmart did not change to match customer expectations and market expectations (like current leading retail stores Walmart and Target) would lead to its inevitable decay into one of the country's largest blighted retail franchises. Antiquated checkout technology equaled longer wait times for customers, a burden they didn't have to deal with at competitor stores. And along Kmart's descent into irrelevance, it simultaneously lost any form of attractiveness for hiring good owners and employers (who wants to work for the country's most outdated store?), leading to even worse customer shopping experiences and corporate management.[10]

Now we fast forward to the year 2017. Silicon Valley is kicking out innovation faster than ever, placing many industries in a constant state of anticipation (or dread depending on where you sit) over the future of their business or organization. Long-held views on how business operates and what will and will not work are constantly being shaken, including those on public transportation.

In 2011, San Francisco was introduced to a new and innovative company called Uber that allowed its customers to hail taxis from the convenience of their smartphones.[11] Uber has been making colossal waves in its field, and it has many taxi drivers and companies on edge (to put it lightly). In 2016, *Slate Magazine* published an article titled "The End of the Taxi Era," which pretty well summarizes the current opinion regarding the taxi

9 Lewis. "Kmart's Ten Deadly Sins."
10 Company Man. "The Decline of Kmart."
11 Hartmans and McAlone. "The Story."

industry. Author Will Oremus begins by stating, "The bankruptcy of San Francisco's largest cab company is just the beginning. Thanks to Uber, the entire industry is doomed."[12] Oremus is referring to San Francisco's (previously) largest taxi company Yellow Cab. While the future is still unknown regarding how the game will end, it is clear that innovation appears to have the upper hand.

It is interesting to point out that, similar to the story of Blockbuster's competition with Netflix, this is not just your standard David and Goliath story line—where the industry favorite towers over the feeble underdog, only to be overcome by the underdog's skull-crushing stone of innovation. In this story, both fighters had rocks chambered in their sling. The difference is that Uber got the rock first.

Before Yellow Cab went under, they threw a Hail Mary pass in an attempt to counter their competitor's attack by creating an app that would allow users to hail a Yellow Cab from their smartphone, in lieu with Uber's strategy. However, by the time they were able to execute this about-face, it was too late. The app was unable to save the company from their downward slide due to their small number of drivers compared to Uber's 20,000 drivers. It would seem that many Yellow Cab drivers had come to the conclusion that they were on a sinking ship, and that it was better to jump ship sooner rather than later. Oremus states, "Those drivers are highly sensitive to changes in the marketplace, making them prone to bolt en masse as it becomes clear which way the wind is blowing."[13] Regardless of opinion on Uber's humanity, the fact is that their business model is beating out their competitors because they innovated from the ground up. It would appear that, in this story,

---

12 Oremus. "The End of the Taxi Era."
13 Oremus

Goliath's difficulty to adjust strategy in time would secure David's win.

I use the stories of Blockbuster, Kmart, and Yellow Cab as lessons to drive home what is at stake if companies do not practice healthy innovation. Innovation is no longer a commodity but rather a necessity. In this chapter, we will discuss both the current state of innovation in our world as well as possible threats that lie in an inability or refusal to innovate.

Comfort Kills

As observed in one's rate of improvement at an activity such as playing an instrument or sport, there comes a point along the procession of the growth curve where the level of energy required to achieve one unit of progress becomes much greater than when the learning curve was less steep. For example, when I started learning to play the guitar, I achieved a large amount of progress in a short amount of time. Now, improvement takes much more effort than it used to when I was first beginning. This point where growth becomes harder to achieve is the point where the draw towards comfort can easily become all-consuming. When a design (or any social impact field, for that matter) hits this point, it becomes all too easy to pursue comfort over progress. After a while, the choice to choose progress becomes almost invisible as apathy takes over, and once apathy has set in, stagnation is likely to follow.

With this said, it is important to note that it would be impossible for anyone to innovate *every* aspect of their work. As we will see throughout the book, the only achievable solution is to innovate in selective areas that are deemed critical for the flourishing of that organization. Find your innovation lane, then stay in it.

Because innovation is happening now faster than ever before, it is critical for innovation to continually be occurring at the macro-level of industries or the chance of falling behind is imminent. For example, in the 20th century, it took landline telephones seventy-five years to achieve fifty million users, airplanes sixty-eight years, and television twenty-two years. Compare that to the 21st century where it took YouTube four years, Facebook three years, and Twitter two years to hit that same benchmark. As if those weren't fast enough, in 2009, it took the Angry Birds app only thirty-five days to achieve that very same fifty million users benchmark.[14]

The rate of technological, economical, and cultural progression is growing at a rapid pace, a phenomenon that has come to be explained with what has become known as Moore's Law. Moore's Law (more of a statistical observation, really) is based upon the observations of Gordon Moore in 1965 when he noticed that the number of transistors scientists were able to fit on one square inch of an integrated circuit board had virtually doubled since the invention's conception.[15] This principle of exponential growth has now come to describe the rapid rate of change experienced in all parts of our world, including business, science, technology, and culture. Technologist expert Reuven Cohen states, "The time it takes to get a job done is constantly decreasing leading to unexpected consequences. The increase in speed and efficiency has become a key business driver enabling businesses to evolve at ever increasing speeds."[16]

> *Find your innovation lane, then stay in it.*

---

14 Ritholtz. "The Pace of Innovation."
15 Cohen. "Business Success Is Happening Faster."
16 Cohen

Even the fashion industry is currently finding itself in the midst of growing pains. With technology and social media in the hands of nearly every buyer, runway shows that used to be privy only to retailers, industry insiders, and the press are now available instantaneously to everyone and their mother, creating a desire and pressure for styles and trends that used to be allowed time before they were introduced to the mainstream market. As a result, experts are finding that newly introduced clothing lines are now being perceived as antiquated and out-of-date by the time they reach the racks.[17]

The fact that trends and developments are becoming outdated faster than ever is made crystal clear in the music industry. In decades past, the term "old school" was used to describe music (depending on the genre) typically from two decades ago or more. Now, with the rate at which styles are changing and tastes are developing, culture (myself included) now looks at music from simply a decade ago as "old school."

This accelerated rate of growth is largely due to both the growing amount of information available to consumers and the speed at which it becomes available. If the Industrial Age* encapsulated the effect of the machine upon society and the Digital Age* that of computers, the Information Age we are in will continue to be marked by greater leaps in our abilities to produce and absorb content in larger amounts and at greater speeds. Companies like Facebook, Tesla, Google, and Apple are leading the charge in the quest to usher the world into all of the possibilities the Information Age offers.

Because of innovation within society, we are now seeing new ways to work, with flexible schedules, more

---

17 Wallace. "New Report Proves."

comfortable furniture, open office spaces, and others. There are new ways to interact socially with online dating apps, such as Tinder and Bumble, and an ever-increasing number of forms of social media, such as Snapchat, Instagram, Twitter, and (old school) Facebook. It's as if we are already aboard Elon Musk's SpaceX rocket ship en route to a distant place never before perceived as attainable, at times giddy with excitement and at other times scared to death we might lose our grip and be lost along the way.

    If that's the current state of innovation, where does that leave SID? Thankfully for us, history has always shown a (somewhat) predictable path upon which the arts and humanities have developed. Before an art movement is formed or an architectural style created, one can always find the embryo of that movement embedded deeply within society long before either was created. This embryo is often referred to as the "zeitgeist"* of the age or "the general intellectual, moral, and cultural climate of an era."[18] While the agents that influence the formation of this climate extend far beyond the capacity and purpose of our discussion, let us suffice it to say that the development in the arts and sciences we are and have been experiencing stem directly from the current zeitgeist of our age. With that understood, one may then begin to understand the leap from a culture's ideology to the expression of that ideology through art, science, architecture, music, and other arts.

    Before the Greeks laid the chisel to the first column of their calm, stoic, and orderly temple, there was the search for meaning, a search that concluded for them in the inherent beauty, wisdom, and value in perfection. Preceding the international style's abhorrence

---

18 Merriam-Webster, s.v. "zeitgeist," accessed 2018. https://www.merriam-webster.com/dictionary/zeitgeist.

of decoration and building components that elevated individuality over conformity, there was war, terrible war, that seemed to arise from the forced domination of one ideology over another. This led to the desperate desire for an architectural expression of peace and equality, resulting in a style free of any major differentiating characteristics.

Where, then, does our current time and zeitgeist leave us? What is one to project regarding the anticipated trajectory of SID? And what effect will that trajectory have upon all social entrepreneurs? Much of that question remains to be answered as only time will tell, yet we can safely assume that it will fall in line with the same currents pushing the acquisition of more and more information.

The Needs
In what ways do SID and social entrepreneurship need to innovate?

As we explored in Chapter 1, SID has been the recipient of the measly scraps that design has left to give as "truly quality design" has been a luxury SID wasn't afforded. Apparently, this injustice has been considered an acceptable loss due to the fact that the road to greater economic success has rarely crossed SID's path. And since financial gain and social impact work have never been neighbors, the tool of innovation has mostly been kept in the hands of the pursuers of wealth rather than social impact.

Yet innovation and SID are not complete strangers.

In 1913, John D. Rockefeller founded the Rockefeller Foundation, innovating the world of philanthropy* by helping people get a hand *up* versus a hand *out*, something that had not yet been effectively created at the global scale. Eric John Abrahamson, Ph.D., writes about the Foundation that "they struggled to shape and maintain an organizational culture that would promote effective philanthropy. They worried constantly about becoming stale or bureaucratic. These efforts helped to sustain in the organization a habit of innovation that defies cliché."[19] The Foundation was built upon innovative practices that, to this day, still ring true as they continue to build upon the global and idealistic ambition to promote the "well-being of mankind."[20]

Unfortunately, this energy and progressive thinking has been absent more often than not in SID, leading to stale and subpar designs that, while good-intentioned and relatively successful in their own regard, stand little chance of rising to the challenges presented by our current era. Richard Hale, leader, trainer, and conultant for non-profit organizations, states, "Perhaps living too long in the world of serving the poor and disenfranchised has made non-profits passive and unwilling to claim their legitimate share of the pie."[21] For social entrepreneurs, this statement still rings true.

So, what are some of the specific issues that we face if innovation is kept away from the social impact table? Two of the most prominent needs and issues I perceive are refugees and the environment:

> 1. With the world's ever-growing capacity to create greater casualties through war and violence, we can expect to see more displaced citizens in need of shelter and destroyed cities and buildings in need of reconstruction. The United Nations (UN) claims that 65.3 million people are currently

---

[19] Abrahamson. *Beyond Charity*.
[20] Abrahamson
[21] Male. "Nonprofit Weaknesses."

either internally or externally displaced. "Refugee camps are becoming storage facilities for people. The average camp stay is 17 years. That's a generation," says former UN Refugee Agency official Kilian Kleinschmidt. "I think we have reached a dead end where the humanitarian agencies cannot cope with the crisis." He goes on to explain that "we're doing humanitarian aid as we did 70 years ago after the Second World War. Nothing has changed."[22] These are urgent needs that social entrepreneurs and designers can have a direct influence upon.

2. The ever-increasing need for more natural resources and the ensuing excretion of its non-biodegradable waste brings the need for good design solutions to protect our limited availability of natural resources. Change in climate is also a factor that must be observed and addressed through good and innovative design solutions.

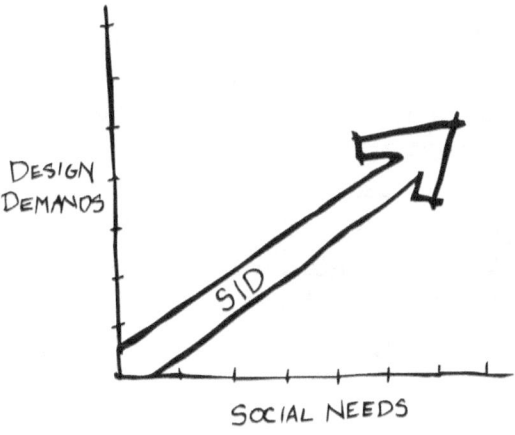

22 Wood. "Emergency Shelter."

Adequate Tools and Skills

I feel the proverbial "bringing the knife to a gun fight" is all too fitting for the future I envision in which social entrepreneurs are not constantly seeking the best and most effective tools and skill sets. Designer and civic entrepreneur Alastair Parvin states, "If we're serious about problems like climate change, urbanization and health, actually, our existing development models aren't going to do it."[23] Parvin is a big proponent of open-source software for the purpose of freely distributing residential designs online that require little tools and can be assembled by two to three people within a day. While Parvin claims "this approach is not innovation,"[24] citing that it was how buildings were built for hundreds of years before the Industrial Revolution, I would dare to object and say the introduction of an old idea through new medium or tool is precisely the type of innovation social entrepreneurs will need both now as well as tomorrow.

      For some, there is a concern regarding the perceived inevitable outcome of the negative effect current SID culture is having upon the future of the field. Architect John Hudson, founder of the international non-profit design firm 100 Fold Studio, claims that without innovation, he fears the realm of SID may become irrelevant due to a lack of licensed architects.[25] While supportive of the causes that many designers in recent years have supported through their immediate response to solving design problems while simultaneously neglecting the industry standard's path to licensure, Hudson claims that even though this path may be appropriate for some,

---

23 Parvin. "Architecture for the People."
24 Parvin
25 John Hudson (Founder, 100 Fold Studio), interviewed by Jacob DeNeui in Battambang, Cambodia, July 14, 2017.

there must be an equally fulfilling and socially impactful path that includes licensure in order to ensure the continued presence of SID professionals that are able to tackle larger scale projects that, in many jurisdictions, require such licensure.[26] And while the specific nature of this conundrum may differ depending on your social impact field, it clearly illustrates the importance for all social entrepreneurs to critically evaluate the tools and skills required for their work, from higher education to technological capacity.

Our discussion of the effectiveness of social impact tools and skills would not be complete without mentioning what we might view as the biggest gun of all: business. Business is defined as "the practice of making one's living by engaging in commerce."[27] There is no way for any contributive member of society to avoid this need to engage in commerce, making business one of the strongest and most powerful forces available in our world. Social impact strategist Wendy Woods states, "The only way we're going to make substantial progress on the challenging problems of our time is for business to drive the solutions."[28] It is important to point out that it is not the purpose of this book to endorse one form of economic mode of operation over another (for-profit vs. non-profit), but rather to present the tools and skills available to social impact entrepreneurs and innovators while allowing them the freedom and autonomy to explore those options which best serve their mission and leaning. We will more fully dive into our discussion of financing SID in Chapter 7.

---

26 John Hudson
27 Encyclopedia.com, s.v. "business," accessed 2018. https://www.encyclopedia.com/social-sciences-and-law/economics-business-and-labor/economics-terms-and-concepts/business-0.
28 Woods. "The Business Benefits of Doing Good."

Millennials
Millennials have now overtaken both the Baby Boomers and Generation X in the workforce, a fact that is not to be taken lightly. In order for organizations to attract new and young talent into their fold, hiring and retention strategies must reflect the desires of the millennials they are looking to hire. While there are many factors that young talent take into consideration when pursuing careers, millennials are more often than not attracted to businesses and organizations that have snagged some slice of the innovative pie.

One benefit that social impact businesses or organizations have over others is that millennials are much more interested than any other generation previous in making social impact a part of their job. Molly Petrilla shared with *Fortune* readers that "millennials have a different view of social responsibility," adding that "while entrepreneurs traditionally built their businesses and wealth first and considered philanthropy later, [millennials] are thinking about their social impact early on."[29] It is apparent that the cultural shift we are witnessing in the current spirit of our age is drawing young millennials away from the traditional climb of the corporate ladder into a more cause-driven career track, and that's really good for social entrepreneurs.

> *"The only way we're going to make substantial progress on the challenging problems of our time is for business to drive the solutions."*
> *- Wendy Woods*

---

29 Petrilla. "'Millennipreneurs'"

One study found that 82 percent of millennials prefer businesses that support the health and wellness of both consumers and employees in their investment portfolio.[30] With a larger number of workers seeking to positively impact society through their chosen trade comes a greater chance for creating change that matters.

However, it is important not to forget that many millennials are simultaneously interested in being on the front line of innovation with their work. This means the failure for social entrepreneurs and organizations to innovate would logically result in decreased desirability in the eyes of some of the most creative and entrepreneurial members of our evolving workforce.

Ain't nobody got time for that.

In Summary...
We saw how the focused application of innovation can keep industries from falling into the comfort trap, examined how our current culture (or zeitgeist) is defined largely in part by the fast and voluminous transfer of information, and examined three specific prompts behind the need to innovate in social impact fields including growing humanitarian and environmental problems, the need for effective tools and skills, and the changing needs and desires of the incoming workforce. With all of this groundwork now laid, we are getting tantalizingly close to tackling the question of how to innovate, but before that, we must first return to our mysterious island so we can see how Sid innovates her way out of danger.

---

30 Coan and Schwartz. "Millennials Demand More."

Chapter 3 in a page...

- Kmart, Blockbuster, and Yellow Cab illustrate how failure to innovate (or innovate effectively) can be deadly in today's day and age.
- Comfort with status quo kills innovation.
- Find your own innovation lane, then stay in it.
- Innovation can solve several needs:
    o Due to human population growth and advances in technology, the increased ability to decimate the environment and ourselves will require more innovative solutions to solve.
    o Social impact fields won't last long in a gun fight with a knife. Innovation can provide the necessary tools and ideas in order to compete with fields typically equipped with greater resources.
    o Social entrepreneurs must attract the best and the brightest of the upcoming workforce. Millennials commonly seek innovative work, meaning SID organizations must provide that or risk losing their desired workforce.

Food for Thought...

1. Think of your field as a whole. Is it known for being stagnant or innovative?
2. Can you think of a problem in your industry or current organization that you think is a result of antiquated ideas?
3. What needs in your industry (i.e., global violence, poverty, increasing environmental damage) do you foresee being the greatest obstacle to your social impact objectives?

Chapter 4

BIRD'S EYE VIEW

"Those who danced looked quite insane to those who didn't hear the music."

— Unknown

(3:41 PM)

A Creative Affair
Sid looked down at the sketchbook that lay atop her petite lap, now nearly completely saturated with ink and moisture from her favorite Staedtler pigment liner mixed with the sprinkling of wet snowflakes she was so fascinated by. She did her best to brush them off to keep her pages from getting wet and crinkling, one of her worst pet peeves, but only succeeded in smearing the once crisply applied ink across the surface of her desperate creativity's platform for holy ideation. Sydney smiled slightly as her mind drifted back on one of her favorite sayings: "Those who danced looked quite insane to those who didn't hear the music." To her, those few words were full of poetry and idealism, two things she most deeply cherished in her life. She also loved to dance. Who was it that said that? Nietzsche perhaps? Or maybe it was one of Mark Twain's golden nuggets? *Eh, doesn't matter*, she thought as she removed the end of her pen from her mouth before her teeth gifted it

with an early end. Those words had brought her peace of mind in many of the situations in life she had found herself in. This was no exception.

For the past few minutes since Will had departed, Sid had been furiously thinking, sketching, and racking her brain for the answer she needed, the life vest that would save her from this icy, menacing predicament. She had become quite skilled over the years at diving into prolonged periods of deeply focused work. Her job required it in order to continually produce design that pushed boundaries and created new ideas and thoughts that had attracted and engaged her customer's clients.

Sid loved her work.

No other profession that she could think of gave a person such unbridled creative freedom while producing such tangible, quantifiable results. She had entered college, now almost ten years ago, without much direction, only a deep love for drawing and no idea whatsoever of what to do with it. After her second semester of graphic design courses, however, she knew she had found her calling. The marriage of art and business seemed to resonate so loudly within the depths of her soul. After her first date with typology, she had fallen hopelessly in love. She found the subtle yet striking power of font design upon the human psyche tantalizing, though she never would have imagined such a fascination before taking the class.

The beautiful part of her newly kindled affair with graphic design was that the honeymoon never seemed to end. There may have been brief moments of disenchantment, but her heart was for design and design alone. Her business and marketing classes strengthened her confidence that she could make a living in this field. As she began learning the art and science of web design, she found not only satisfaction from the work but also the great job security it promised due to the world's endless supply of businesses and organizations who could use the work she offered.

It was a match made in heaven.

There was one aspect of the field that solidified their heavenly fidelity. Sid had always been a problem solver from day one. She had to chuckle to herself as she thought back to her grand design for a contraption that could quietly open the cookie jar and transfer its contents to her conniving hands all without alerting her mother. One of her favorite childhood "inventions" was her brilliantly philanthropic idea of creating a long vacuum tube (much like the ones at the bank) that would quickly transport all of her nutritious/disgusting dinner leftovers through a small slot in her kitchen wall to the left of the sink, across the Atlantic Ocean, and straight into the open mouth of a hungry child in Africa. She couldn't help but laugh as she recalled how proud she was of her brilliant idea and how she had tearfully questioned her mother's humanity when she refused to begin work on the project by cutting a hole in the wall immediately.

Sid had always been a problem solver, and design's most irresistible dowry to her was the power and fortitude to solve any problem she faced.

It's why Sid had always had a hard time accepting status quo solutions to problems. She had hated school most of her childhood because of how the system had strapped her down for twelve years and force-fed her with pre-digested facts and bits of information that someone else had chewed on, spit out, and passed along to a teacher who found it morally acceptable to regurgitate these bile-soaked messages into her strong-willed mind.

Sid cringed at the mere thought of those troubling times.

But those days were long gone now that she had found her match. With design, she had come to feel that the whole world was at her fingertips. During her brief career, she had already worked with numerous clients involved in a wide array of products including steel construction materials, baby formula, feminine hygiene products, and perhaps the most interesting, a Japanese cryotherapy sauna. Each client had a specific and unique marketing need that always required her creativity and imagination to their fullest extent. Sometimes the budgets had been tight and the timelines even tighter, but Sid had never failed to meet the expectations of her clients.

Which is why she now found it so challenging to withstand the icy chill of Peter and Will's lack of faith in her ability to find the solution. The disappointment had been gnawing in the back of her mind ever since Peter set off, and now Will too had placed his vote of no confidence in her.

Maybe I'm trying to fix something that isn't broken, she thought as she placed her pen in the crease between the two blank pages, gently closing the book and setting it back safely in her pack so she could stand up. As she slowly rose, she clenched her jaw and humbly absorbed the knives that now violently stabbed into her side. "I know of at least two things that are most definitely broken," she quietly muttered through gritted teeth. She fought to hold in the pain as she focused on controlling her breathing.

It helped, but not much.

Exploration

Was she really trying to reinvent the wheel like Will had

said? Both he and Peter had been firmly set on taking the most apparently logical route by going back to the ship to try to catch up to everyone else. They had figured that they could simply add some mustard to their hustle in order to get back in time. Yet here she was, still sitting in the same place for the past half hour as she ran through scenario after scenario, trying to wrap her mind around the idea that was struggling to be brought to light.

First, she considered making her way up to the precariously perched ledge not more than three hundred feet up the mountain slope they had been about to summit before the quake. But she knew that would take at least another hour, and with the visibility continuing to diminish, the odds of seeing anything were slim to none.

She too had contemplated heading back the way they came from, much like Peter and Will, but abandoned that idea quickly after thinking about the minimal odds of reaching the team before they pulled anchor and left the harbor. Next, she thought about pulling a MacGyver and jury-rigging some kind of signal fire there on top of the mountain with all of the flares, fire paste (i.e., secret sauce for underachieving fire starters), and flint she still had in her pack. This idea had excited her the most out of all of them, but after thinking about how much fuel it would take for the signal to be seen, she quickly abandoned the idea upon surveying the landscape and failing to find any significant form of vegetation, save for the miniscule amounts of alpine moss that clung to the rocks that weren't quite covered in snow yet. Though beautiful in all of their brilliant oranges and natural greens, they would serve little good as fire starter. And now without Peter or Will to help gather wood from far away, the odds of that working were even fewer.

    Sidney warmed her cold body, moving her limbs back and forth while trying not to remind her body of its numerous injuries. As she began to walk away from her idea throne (that's what she called anything that she sat on while designing), sketchbook in hand, she slowly twisted her water bladder's plastic tube to break up the ice in order to take a few sips of water out of the rubbery mouthpiece she had attached to the front of her rucksack straps for ease of reach. As she sipped, her eyes gazed upward, searching for some form of inspiration, some guiding light to lead her to the solution she sought. "Or just a freakin' bird would be acceptable right now," she grumbled as she spit the rubber from her mouth, "anything but this wet blanket of a skyline."

    That's when she thought she saw something, there, through the clouds and snow. As her eyes strained westward down the slope, wondering if she had imagined it—No! There it was again! Through a small but perceivable break in the clouds, Sid could vaguely make out what appeared to be the dark, lush green of the jungle. It was a part of the island they had not yet explored, though she quickly realized it was the section they saw first when they discovered land just four days ago.

    The team had been understandably elated at finding the island and, in their excitement, either Peter or Rita had suggested anchoring right away and embarking upon their exploration immediately. Carlos considered the idea but chose to veto the decision. The team later unanimously agreed with the decision upon discovering the much more spacious and sheltered Dragon's Tail Harbor, as they called it. Carlos had explained that this coast was much too exposed to the stormy gales that had continuously battered them from the northwest. And while there was certainly an abundant number of dead logs that would be a great source of firewood, the short length of available beach line below the trees was covered mostly in small- to medium-sized boulders covered in barnacles and seaweed, which would not make it the most ideal site for comfortable sleeping quarters over the next several days of their exploration.

The beach was also quite steep, though ultimately this was a fact that delighted the team, for beyond the sharp embankment and through the steeply packed wall of lush jungle lay a beautiful snow-capped mountain. "We should call it Mount Franklin, like in The Mysterious Island!" Rita had excitedly suggested upon Carlos's invitation for names. By now, all of them had read Jules Verne's novel at least twice, and they were none too eager to commemorate his inspiring piece of literature by imitating Verne's choice of names his characters had given their own mysterious island. Despite their eagerness to discover more of the mountain (it was still far away and covered in low-hanging clouds), Carlos reminded them that the first priority would be to find a suitable place to lay anchor.

So, the team had continued on, hugging the island's coastline as they headed east. With the occasional interruption of a larger boulder, the terrain remained relatively unchanged as they sailed along, though the distance from the water to the tree line varied anywhere from nothing to a few yards. However, no suitable harbor was to be found.

Carlos had tasked Sid with creating the map of the island, and she had eagerly accepted, doing her best to picture the island as if she was a bird sailing high above the boat, looking down upon the entire island, a real "bird's-eye view." As Sid's imagination had continued to sail, so too did the Wild Blue Yonder (the name she had given their brave vessel of exploration) as she continued along the coastline. After Sid had finished her very best iteration of what she presumed the island to be like, she looked down upon her work and laughed at what looked like a petite little revolver, seemingly aimed at the open ocean they had just crossed to get to the island. "It's like cloud-gazing," she whispered reflectively, once again lost in her imagination, transported to her beloved world of make-believe and paper, magic and ink.

    About three quarters of the way along the southern coast, they discovered Dragon's Tail Harbor snuggled up inside the island as if the mythical beast had tired of the barraging winds and pulled itself into the island to seek shelter. The sandy beach and protection from the elements quickly led the entire team to pick this as the most logical and ideal place for camp, yet they agreed it would be best to continue surveying the coast first since there was still much daylight left and they wanted to explore the outer edges (Sid, in particular, since she was determined to finish the outline of her map).

    So continue they did, carried along by the favorable western winds as they began to slowly make their way up the eastern coast. The going was slow due to the fact that they were forced to swing farther out into the water another sixty or seventy yards beyond the east coastline in order to avoid the shallow ground and what appeared to be large, hull-gouging, razor-like boulders that protruded menacingly from the water. Though far from view, Sid could still vaguely make out the beautiful coastline they were now forced to view from afar through a minefield of what she called "dragon scales." Sid hoped to be able to walk along the coast once they anchored elsewhere.

    Once Carlos deemed it safe to proceed closer to the coast, the sky was beginning to darken slightly as the sun began to descend below the crowns of the jungle trees to their left, so they made the decision to continue exploring the rest of island's coastline upon their departure. Sid felt satisfied with what she had been able to ascertain regarding the island's perimeter, having ended with the wonderful, pebble-strewn section of beach to the northeast tip of the island.

    "Yet another spot I can't wait to see," she remarked to the group. The whole boat had been filled with excitement that day, she remembered, as their minds were filled with wondrous thoughts of what lay ahead of them. They had come fully prepared for all conditions, including snow and ice, which had allowed them to set out in confidence three days later for the snow-laden Mount Franklin they had but glimpsed. As Sid recalled, the whole team had spoken almost exclusively about how excited they were to get to the mountain as they turned and sailed back the way they came, around the dragon scales and back into Dragon's Tail Harbor.

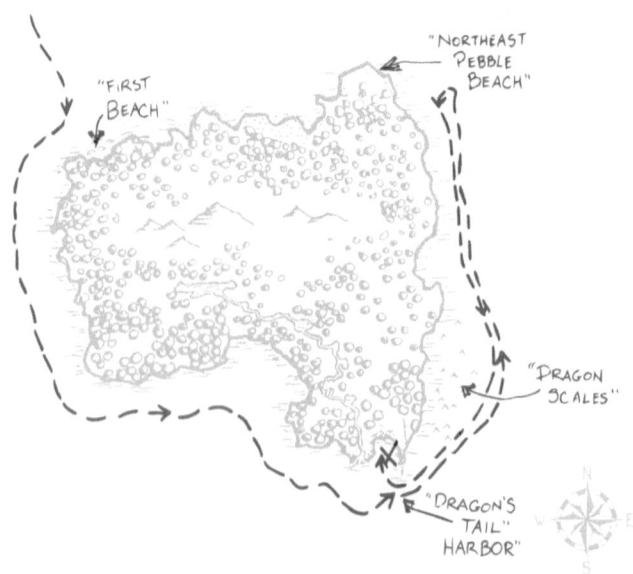

A Bird's-Eye View
Now these thoughts seemed to be but distant memories as Sid stood with her eyes locked on that narrow aperture of jungle that lay below and beyond her, perhaps another three to five miles. She was thankful the snow had temporarily stopped falling, long enough for her to look back upon the island's western face. And as she continued to stare, it was as if heaven itself breathed down through the mist and the clouds she now looked upon, opening up her view even of what lay beyond. With delight, she could see the previously hidden afternoon sun begin to peak through, clearing away what had been hidden from view until now. As she stood there admiring the view, temporarily forgetting the moment's urgency, she suddenly felt a ray of sunshine pierce through the clouds and gently dance across her cold, wind-burnt face.

    She closed her eyes and smiled.

    It was as if, in this brief moment, nature's song was being sung, and the sun was dancing in step. And as she stood there, mesmerized by the light that now graciously touched her face, whispering in her ears, her mind was once again transported upwards. She was a bird, soaring free and high in the sky, as if nothing else mattered except this moment, here, now, this beautiful dance. As she soared, she looked down at the mountain and strangely saw herself standing there, looking up at her bird self. Then, to her delight, as her wings carried her farther west into the setting sun, she must have been transported back in time, for there below her was the Wild Blue Yonder, sailing upon the blue waters. It was as if the boat was following her flight as she continued to sail west away from the shore and into—

    Wait.

Why was the boat sailing west? If she was truly imagining the past, they would have been sailing east, toward the island. Yet here they were leaving the island, hugging the coastline as they had on their initial arrival days earlier.

Suddenly, Sid was no longer flying high above the clouds with the ship below her and the island behind her, but once again found herself back home in her body, but now her eyes were wide open, wider than they'd ever been perhaps.

"That's it!" she shrieked. Almost tripping over her own legs in excitement, she began to sprint downward and westward as fast as her legs would carry her (that is until she realized the weight of her epiphany had replaced that of her pack, forcing her to quickly retrace her steps, grab her gear, and then set out once more down the snowy slope). The pain in her side no longer slowed her down as she felt the warmth of the fire that had now been lit within her spirit.

Or perhaps it was the sun still shining down upon her through the beautiful break in the clouds.

(3:53 PM)

Interception

As she descended past boulder after ever-increasing boulder, Sid excitedly continued to put together her plan.

How could I have not thought of this before?! she thought. Well, regardless, she now knew how she was going to make all things right.

Sid was going to intercept her team.

It had taken a nearly psychedelic bird episode for her to conclude one thing: the only way she could be sure to find the team again would be to intercept them along the northwestern coastline before they pushed away and set off for their homes. In an instant, she knew that this was the only logical path they would take for several reasons. First, the extra sixty or seventy yards they would have had to travel in order to avoid the dragon scales would have added unnecessary time to their trip. Plus, if they wanted to finish charting the island's perimeter from the safety of the boat, it would have made the most sense to approach from the west (though she doubted any of them would still be interested in exploring after thinking that three of their teammates had just been lost). Finally, hugging the southern coast would leave them temporarily sheltered from the northwest head winds they had previously so appreciated during their arrival.

Sid began to slow her descent as the path that had previously been ice sprinkled with rocks had now become rocks sprinkled with ice. As she stopped to catch her breath and remove her ice crampons from her well-worn hiking boots, she could clearly see the edge of the jungle and the water's edge just beyond. She estimated it was still two to two and a half miles away but at least 1,000 feet below. The ever-steepening pitch of the mountain now forced her to slow her pace considerably as she continued her descent. Occasionally, she was forced to her hands and knees when the terrain became too steep to safely take on just two feet.

After forty-five minutes of arduous and sometimes treacherous advancement, she descended the beautiful and rugged western face of Mount Franklin, arriving once again at the border of the island's lush and verdant jungle. There, she afforded herself one more quick respite to her quivering lungs and throbbing ribcage. Despite her situation's urgency, she couldn't help but simultaneously soak in the majesty of her surroundings. As she turned to look back upon the icy mountain she had just traversed, now completely radiant in the golds and reds of the reflecting light of the setting sun, she let her eyes close softly as she felt her spirit warm once again. The jungle's trees now left her in shadows, but her optimism could not be darkened. It was no more than a minute, but a minute was all she needed to refresh her vigor and focus on the task at hand. While it left her feeling nearly intoxicated, her clarity could not be dulled as she once again set off to accomplish her mission.

(5:23 PM)

Light at the End of the Jungle
Though not as steep as her previous free-climbing adventure, the foliage was thick and heavy, at times almost impenetrable. Sid was thankful for the light her headlamp now afforded her as the crown of the trees blocked out most of the fading light, casting deep and dark shadows over her and everything around. Despite the toilsome work it was slicing through the nearly impenetrable living wall, she persevered, trying to somehow keep one hand on her side while using the other to hack through the vines and leaves with her ice ax.

Save for an occasional clearing, normally brought about by a large boulder that forced her to retrace her steps and descend a different way, the scenery did not change much until nearly thirty minutes of hacking, sawing, grimacing, and angry temper tantruming later when she detected the soft splash of the ocean waves upon the shore. With a click, she extinguished the now dispensable light from her headlamp as the trees before her began to thin, bowing to the power of the setting golden sun. Finally, after what seemed like decades, her eyes confirmed what her ears had prophesied, and she could scarce contain herself: before her now lay the beach.

Thankfully, not all of her previous escape iterations had been in vain. Where the signal fire would have been useless from atop the mountain, the northwestern beach would be the perfect place for a signal fire. She realized now that all of the dead wood Carlos had pointed out earlier when they had initially surveyed the beach would be exactly what she needed if she was to light a signal that would shine bright enough to be seen by the team as they left in the boat. The fact that the sun was setting was actually quite fortuitous since her fire would be much more visible in the dark than in the daylight. Having already reviewed the fire starter contents of her pack, she knew she had just enough fire paste, flint, and steel to get the fire going.

After entering the jungle, Sid had immediately started gathering dry underbrush, stuffing all of her available coat pocket space with the perfect tinder she would need to ignite her little bonfire. Now as she stood on the beach looking out upon the endless ocean before her with perfectly dry fire-starting material in hand, she smiled to herself. She only wished she had brought some marshmallows and graham crackers to make a party out of it.

(6:03 PM)

Fire Dancing

Barnacles and broken seashells pressed into Sid's hands and knees as she kneeled in front of the small Lincoln Log-like structure that lay before her, no bigger than her favorite bean bag she enjoyed so much back home. She had carefully laid the gnarled, dried-out driftwood in a neat stack, filling it with the dry underbrush she had previously gathered, adorning it all with a greasy bead of fire paste that snaked across the top of the pile. It was a cute little structure that any young boy or girl would have loved to play with.

She just wanted to watch it burn.

The moisture in the air that had previously disappeared was now back but in the form of a light drizzling rain. Sid had done her very best to protect her wood structure from the fire-killing moisture. Now, she kneeled before the small cabin she had created, flint in one hand and steel in the other, praying it would light. The wind had picked up once she had crossed through the trees and stepped foot on the rocky beach, yet another factor not in her favor. Ever the thinker, Sid had managed to create a surprisingly effective wind block out of the long, thick driftwood she had dragged from every which way and stacked into a tall pile, up to about her waist. She couldn't afford to run out of fuel, so she made sure she was well prepared before lighting the first flame. She would likely only have one chance to make this work, so she wasn't taking any chances.

With a deep breath, she began to scrape the flint against the steel repeatedly, sending tiny little sparks into her little doll house. "Burn baby, come on. Burn!" Finally, after about the tenth strike, she saw a tiny flame begin to rise from the pile. Excitedly, she stooped down again with her chin almost touching the stone to gently blow across the base of her small fire pit. Slowly she blew; slowly the flames grew. The smoke was thick and black from the moisture that had fallen, so she was careful not to blow too hard and thus smother her little baby.

But grow it did until the whole cabin began to glow with flame. She added larger and larger kindling atop her growing flames until the flames reached high into the quickly darkening night sky.

Pride swelled within her and across her face, which was now aglow in the flickering light of her survival masterpiece. She wished she had a volleyball named Wilson. Then, in the best Tom Hanks voice she could channel, she shouted, "Look what I have created! I! I have made—" However, with one emphatic beating of her chest and its subsequent fiery pain in her side, her role play came to an abrupt halt. She half laughed, half cried as she imagined her ribs whispering menacingly to her, "Did you forget what you did to us in that crevasse earlier? Because we didn't."

All the pain in the world could not keep her from laughing in the light of the roaring flames that now proclaimed her existence to her comrades. Sure enough, within fifteen minutes of lighting her fire, she looked out upon the water with delight as a bright flare from afar caught her eye. The plan had worked. Carlos and Rita had found her, which meant that the three of them could then work together to find Peter and Will, wherever they had ended up. Sid was sure her spirit had never felt so much elation, so much hope as she did in that moment.

So she danced.

It didn't matter that Peter and Will hadn't heard the music that she heard all around her, moving her, inspiring her to keep dancing, to keep thinking. As she spun around the fireplace, her mud-soaked boots scraping the rocks beneath her as her eyes traced the stars above her, she breathed deeply, then exhaled fully. To Sid, design was joy. It was power. Now more than ever, she felt empowered to do anything she set her mind to. If this fantastically tumultuous journey had taught her anything, it was that there was no mountain she could not climb, no obstacle she could not overcome (no icy crevasse she couldn't escape), when she embraced who she was designed to be: a designer.

And so she danced.

(7:11 PM)

Ch. 4: Bird's Eye View

CASE STUDY
with Caleb Walker

COMPANY TYPE	Sub-S LLC
YEAR FOUNDED	2011
LOCATION	Bozeman, Montana
ESTIMATED REVENUE	Unknown
APPROXIMATE NUMBER OF EMPLOYEES	35-40[1]

Impact

If you're fortunate enough to be a Bozeman resident (I'm shamelessly biased), you've probably experienced several of the great coffee shops around this Montana town. There are plenty of places to enjoy a cup of joe in a cool, hip environment for such a small town of 45,000. However, if you ask the locals where to go for quality hot drink and a power source in a spacious, enjoyable work environment, many Bozemanites will probably tell you to check out either of Cold Smoke Coffeehouse's two locations. However, there's a lot more to Cold Smoke than meets the eye—a deeply rooted paradigm that people really matter in a market as seemingly unconcerned with philosophy as coffee acting as a significant agent of social impact.

When you first see Caleb Walker, the founder and owner of Cold Smoke, you might assume he is just another one of their many loyal customers. One would

---

[1] All direct quotes in this case study, as well as information about Cold Smoke Coffeehouse, are from the following source: Caleb Walker (Founder, Cold Smoke Coffeehouse), interviewed by Jacob DeNeui in Bozeman, MT, 10-11-2017.

be hard-pressed to not be instantly put at ease by his casual attire and contagiously cheerful spirit. Despite his humble appearance, Walker still manages to successfully run one of the area's favorite coffee shops, and he does it with grace. A Montana native, Walker found that, after simultaneously receiving his master's degree in theology and acquiring his refined taste and respect for good coffee in the American metropolitan cultural hub of Portland, he was homesick for Montana. So in 2011, Walker relocated his family to Bozeman, Montana, and embarked on his dream for a craft coffee hub.

Walker sees his for-profit business as more than a means to make money but also a way to make an impact in the world. "We wanted to be a company that regularly gave back. That's morphed over the years, what that looks like, but we've done it since we started, and we've continued to do it." Since its inception, Cold Smoke has regularly invested in clean water in countries from which they purchase coffee. (One can see a sign in their store that says "Buy Coffee. Give Water.") However, Walker is very intentional about not making this merely a superficial marketing scheme. "We don't talk about it a ton in our community because we haven't wanted that to be the forefront of why people buy coffee here," instead choosing to focus on providing a quality coffee product that supported an intrinsically philanthropic business model instead of relying on customer's pity and charity to support a less than outstanding product. Since Cold Smoke operates with the belief that people have high value regardless of their race, religion, or status in society, they see their work as an opportunity to demonstrate that by selling a product of equally high value. "Whoever comes through that front door, they all have a story, and they all want to be known as a human first rather than what they do, what family do they come from, what their social status is. I could really give a rip about that."

Cold Smoke also thinks their coffee and the space in which their customers purchase and consume it should speak of the same value. That's what makes the experience at Cold Smoke so different from most coffee shops. In developing Cold Smoke's business plan, Walker intentionally budgeted for the design and maintenance of shops that are notably larger than most coffee shops. You may also notice that, unlike many coffee shops, it's no problem finding a power outlet (the bane of our electronics-driven society). "Our goal is to foster community. We encourage people to loiter. Our goal is to serve you as a customer, and that includes more than just 'did you have a positive experience at the register' and 'did you get the right product?'"

Story
So why did I decide to talk about Cold Smoke Coffeehouse and not any of the other great coffee shops around? While I will exclude the highly debated discussion of coffee quality to the coffee connoisseurs (I'm not old enough to like coffee yet), what I can highlight is how one man, armed with a value for human life and quality coffee, made a choice to relocate his family from one of America's biggest culture hubs to a small Montana town. "Our innovativeness came out of a desire for things we saw were lacking in Bozeman. We really felt we saw a void in Bozeman for craft coffee."

Innovation
How many entrepreneurs would move forward with an architectural design for their business when all of their consultants said it was so big they would go bankrupt within one year? Well, I know of at least one. When

Walker proposed building a coffee shop that was three times that of your average coffee shop, his advisors baulked at the idea and tried to convince him that to do so would be entrepreneurial suicide.

But Walker wasn't finished.

He also proposed wiring 600 amps of power to the building. That's, again, three times the normal average. But these numbers were far from afterthoughts for Walker. He knew the awkwardness common in most coffee shops that came from cramped quarters while trying to have intimate conversations. "Because of the size of most coffee shops, it can be awkward sitting so close to someone you don't know that you don't want to hear your conversation." So, he stuck to his guns and held fast to his conviction that he needed more space and available power amenities in order to achieve a socially impactful business that preached a message of equality simply through product and space. Cold Smoke's two locations boast a spacious 4,900 and 7,200 square feet along with 140 and 188 receptacles. Every booth has an outlet, and other outlets through the shop are spaced at four feet apart.

Cold Smoke may not be on the cover of *Forbes* for being the most innovative company of the year any time soon, but it is on the periphery of the adjacent possible* in regards to social impact in some important ways. (The adjacent possible refers to the region just beyond what is currently cutting edge.) Though "donation from profit" charity may be a more standard industry practice, Cold Smoke's business model shows how such standard practices can be paired with more outside-the-box practices such as tripling the amount of available electric receptacles in a seemingly typical coffee shop in order to synergistically create a socially impactful business enterprise.

Advice
- **Trust Yourself**
    - "Now you've got to be smart, but if there's something you feel very strongly about and you just can't shake it, do it." As was the case with Walker, there will be times when common wisdom would preach innovation's antithesis, which is all the more reason to push through. If you've done your research, asked the experts, and still can't shake the feeling that the thing everyone is telling you not to do is exactly what you must do, you should ultimately go with your heart.
- **Get close to the cliff, but not too close.**
    - "We are one decision away from disaster because we kind of walk on the cliff. We have to be cautious about how close we get to the cliff because you can't do everything that is innovative." Walker shared that there are still ideas he would like to implement into his business model but has restrained from doing so for fear that it would be too much to handle. Cold Smoke has picked its "edge," and it is important to use extreme discretion in knowing where, when, and how to innovate.

Chapter 5

PICKLE ICE CREAM SUNDAE

"You cannot achieve a new goal by applying the same level of thinking that got you where you are today."
— Albert Einstein

Let's Start at the Very Beginning...
Instead of sacrificing prudence for haste like Peter or misconstruing intentionality as strategy like Will, Sid took a different approach, a more innovative approach. While the analogy of the out-of-body experience Sid had might seem a bit too mystical and over the top, it is symbolic of this book's core message that all social entrepreneurs contain the creativity necessary to innovatively design their organizations.

Now that we've walked through the need for innovation and seen the obstacles that lie ahead if we don't, we can begin to unpack the meaning of "design before you design" as we explore how social entrepreneurs can apply design processes in the formation of their organization before embarking upon their work.

> *All social entrepreneurs contain the creativity necessary to innovatively design their organization.*

Tim Brown, author of the book *Change by Design*, calls it "moving from the organization of design to the design of organizations."[1]

In this chapter, we will discuss the basics of the design process and learn some very useful tools that can be used in designing your organization. The basics can be broken down in three steps:

1. PROBLEM vs. NEED
2. ROADBLOCKS to OPPORTUNITIES
3. EXPLORE, then COMMIT

Problem vs. Need

A Tainted Concoction
Have you ever had someone, with all the best intentions, share with you what they concluded was the perfect solution to whatever issue you were currently facing? "What you need to do is just get this degree." "You'd solve the issue if you just got this job." "You two would be so perfect together!"

Why is it that these proposed solutions so often fail to address the root of the problem? The answer is that we are our own worst enemy, debilitated by our own shortsightedness and inability to holistically perceive the world. This inability brings with it the unfortunate side effect of often misinterpreting the root issue due to our limited perception. It is this limited perception that, when exposed to a **problem**, can quickly lead to an undeveloped and ill-informed **solution**. In all fairness, the solutions we develop would probably make sense a lot of the time if the world was exactly the way

---

1 Brown. *Change by Design*.

we understood it to be. However, we are all too often shown that we lack sufficient awareness of reality as a whole. We will discuss this important part of solution design more thoroughly in this chapter, but for now, suffice it to say that it is important to focus our attention as designers on the "**problem**" rather than the "**need**."

If you're a social entrepreneur, you probably have an enhanced awareness of the broken parts of our world: education that needs reform, homeless vets who need shelter, wilderness that needs protection. Whatever problem your unique wiring draws your attention to, I'm sure you see that broken part very clearly. And you see it needs fixing.

There are two ways to describe that broken part, and they both have substantially different connotations. Often times it is the **problem**, not the **need**, which we perceive. The key distinction between the two is that the **need** describes the objective gap in the world which needs filling whereas the **problem** carries with it our own pre-conceived (and often false) conception of what the solution to the problem should be. It takes great discernment and patience to separate the two by recognizing which of your unsupported understandings would turn your proposed solution into a tainted concoction.

> *We are our own worst enemy, debilitated by our own shortsightedness and inability to holistically perceive the world.*

Forest for the Trees

Often when we seek to solve a problem, much like Will, we find ourselves constrained by a limited capacity of perception. It's like the age-old proverb: Two blind men come across an elephant for the very first time. After stumbling toward the great beast, seeking to comprehend it by touching the minute percentage available directly in front of them, they each seek to come to an agreement regarding how to describe the elephant yet to no avail. The one closest to the tusk says the elephant is composed of long and curved bone-like material while the man closest to the tail says it is rather thin and leathery with a wisp of hair at the end.

  The proverb serves to illustrate our skewed and often confined point of view due simply to the physical constraints upon our bodies and our minds to perceive reality. Think, for example, of the literal concept of the word *perspective*. Perspective is defined as "the state of existing in space before the eye."[2] As an architect, I spent a great deal of time learning to draw constructed space in the strange phenomenon we call *perspective*. It really is an odd phenomenon if you think about it. Because our two eyes are a mere matter of inches apart from each other and our bodies are not equipped with mechanisms with which to perceive any object from all points of view, the ability to perceive spatial reality is inherently flawed.

  This struggle to represent spatial perception accurately to others can be illustrated by asking ten people to take pictures of any object such as a tree. Without mandating that the viewer stand at a certain place to take the picture at a certain angle, you are likely to receive ten very different pictures, even though they are all visual representations of the same physical object. Between all of the pictures being taken, the concrete reality of the object never fluctuated, yet it is still per-

---

[2] Dictionary.com, s.v. "perspective," accessed 2018. https://www.dictionary.com/browse/perspective.

ceived in different ways.

In much the same way, we often approach problems as if we were photographing the tree from six inches away. It is certainly an interesting composition, revealing the beautiful textures and layers upon layers of cellulose intricately expressed in various, earthy colors and tones. Fascinating as this exploration may be, it does very little for us in our attempt to understand the tree as a whole.

Then we look at the photograph snapped six feet away. Depending on the size of the tree, we now begin to understand more of the macrocosm of the tree such as its relatively rectilinear, vertical frame, its multiple large root components that seem to dive and disappear into the soil. Perhaps you might also be able to view some of its thick branches beginning to protrude from its strong, barky shaft, but you're likely still too close to see that.

Now we step back sixty feet. Most likely, you can now see the tree in its entirety, roots, trunk, branches, and crown. It is now easy to see its spatial relationship with neighboring flora in the surrounding area (seeing the forest now for the trees). In fact, the farther back you step, the more and more you can begin to perceive interactions and relationship between various components and systems at larger and larger scales.

Faster Horse

Let's jump back into our discussion of discerning the **problem** from the **need**. If you had to pick one person within the past 150 years who you felt revolutionized the world the most, who would it be? One of those candidates would undoubtedly have to be Henry Ford, the man credited with revolutionizing the availability of the early automobile. By adapting the assembly line process, Ford maximized efficiency to create a minimal price point, allowing cars to be available and affordable to the average American.[3] What was it that led Ford to create such a gargantuan ripple in the timeline of humanity? Ford had the ability to step back and view the situation from a removed point of view.

If we were to ask ourselves what might have happened had Mr. Ford not chosen to view his design prompt through the lens of innovation but rather through the lens of what the rest of the world thought it needed, we find he answered our question for us when he (supposedly) stated, "If I'd asked my customers what they wanted, they'd have said 'a faster horse'."[4] Tim Brown, CEO and president of the internationally renowned design consultancy IDEO, states that such limited and conventional methods of creating solutions "will never lead to those rule-breaking, game-changing, paradigm-shifting breakthroughs that leave us scratching our heads and wondering why nobody ever thought of them before."[5] Only once we rise above the fog of preconception will we discover solutions to our limited understanding.

3 Vlaskovits. "Henry Ford."
4 Vlaskovits
5 Brown

Roadblocks to Opportunities
Jumping the Tree

Discerning the need is just the first step in designing your solution. Once you've pinpointed the need, it's time to acknowledge the roadblocks. Roadblocks are any challenge that stands between you and your objective: lack of funding, not enough time, inadequate training, and the absence of strategic relationships are all examples of possible roadblocks you might face in your entrepreneurial journey. Yet it is precisely these roadblocks that have propelled so many into exploring roads they might never have traveled down had the challenges not forced them to do so.

The key to turning roadblocks into opportunities is all about approach. When one encounters a roadblock, one of three things is created: **destruction**, **apathy**, or **innovation**. Think of it this way: three mountain bikers are riding down a steep and winding mountain trail (at different times) only to discover a tree fallen across the trail. The first, going so fast he is unable to stop, crashes into the tree and is thrown from his bike—destruction. The second, riding the brakes all the way down, encounters the tree, gets off the bike to survey it, and gloomily concludes there is no hope of finishing his ride—apathy.

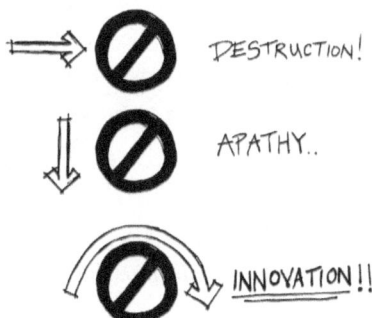

The third rider approaches the tree and chooses instead to pop a wheelie and bunny hop over the log, then continues his ride—innovation.

The first rider is like Blockbuster or Peter from our story. After having ingrained certain habits or paradigms into their lives from doing things a certain way for so long, the very force and power which had helped them dominate in life before became the force that would eventually keep them from future success.

The second rider is every entrepreneur who realized their sword was smaller than Goliath's. They saw that the rules of the game were stacked against them, and so they decided defeat was inevitable. Will might not have been as brash or set in his ways as Peter, but his apathetic adherence to status quo blinded him from the optimal solution that lay just beyond the border of the typical.

Only once we rise above the fog of preconception will we discover solutions to our limited understanding.

It is the third rider who, like Sid, Netflix, and Henry Ford, saw the log not as a deterrent but rather a casting call for Red Bull. Instead of worrying about the size of Goliath's sword, they matched his sword and raised him a slingshot. Instead of playing according to someone else's rules, they made their own rules. The American Revolution would have never been won if the Yankees had fought the British in the way war had always been fought up until that point. In the same way, social impact organizations will never take hold of breathtaking, innovative results if they continue to be made exactly the same way they've been made since forever.

Blind Luck

Architect Chris Downey is a perfect example of this choice. Downey works as an architect and consultant for projects including eye centers, rehabilitation buildings, and transportation projects. Chris is very good at what he does.

Chris is also blind.

After receiving surgery to remove a brain tumor, Downey lost his sight. But what some saw as an insurmountable obstacle in his career, Downey saw as an opportunity to innovate his future. After losing his sight in 2008, Downey went on to found his own consulting firm called Architecture for the Blind. He no longer does the "typical" architect tasks that he used to do before his blindness. Instead, he has found work for which he is uniquely suited. Downey's work, amongst other things, focuses on providing multi-sensory design concepts that set him apart from many architects who have not had to face the same challenges as him. Things he might never have noticed before 2008, such as the warmth and ergonomics of handrails or the joys of enticing smells and sounds, are now unique focuses of his in the services he offers his clients. As he puts it, the way he recovered from the bad deal he was dealt was by "embracing the challenge."[6]

> *Instead of playing according to someone else's rules, they made their own rules.*

Progressive Recession

6 AIANational. "An Architect's Story."

In 2008, workers across the world were struck by a financial recession that left many without work or jobs, including many designers. While the typical reaction to such hardship would be to quit pursuing work in the design field due to its being one of the first services to skim during financial difficulties (apathy), many used it as an opportunity to pursue socially impactful work they had long had a passion for, including John Hudson. While Hudson had been allowing the idea for 100 Fold Studio to percolate within his mind for around ten years prior to the recession, it was the lack of available work in his hometown of Birmingham, Alabama, that was the final factor that prompted John and his family to pack up their belongings and head North to Montana in order to start their innovative non-profit architecture firm.

One out of 200
If anyone knows how to create innovation soup out of nothing, it's Bobby Gruenewald. One day while standing in the TSA line at the Chicago/O'Hare airport, Gruenewald, the innovation pastor at Life.Church, wondered if there was some way to help him read the Bible more than his busy schedule seemed to be allowing him. That's when the idea for what would become the most popular Bible app came to him. When he presented his idea for posting the entire Bible for free on the internet to the church staff members, he was given permission to begin prototyping but only with the knowledge that there was simply no budget of time or finances available for the project.
    Talk about a roadblock.
    Thankfully, Gruenewald is one of those guys who actually finds constraints appealing. In fact he goes so far as to say, "People want to think outside the box, but it's actually embracing the box. If you had more resourc-

es you would just buy a solution. You wouldn't need to innovate."⁷ With no budget, no time, and no connections within the publishing industry (ends up someone besides God owns the legal rights to the Bible), Gruenewald set out to create a solution for the **need** he saw for people to have faster and easier access to the Bible.

He addressed the first roadblock of time and budget by finding volunteers, like himself, who were just excited about the idea and would work on it outside of their normal 8–5. The next hurdle he had to overcome was how to convince the publishers to give him their intellectectual property—for free. This was where Gruenewald took advantage of the current shift in retail culture toward the elimination of the "middle man" by pursuing a more direct relationship with the customer. Publishing industries were all too aware of the looming extinction of retail stores, the ones that had historically done the work of drawing their customers to their products. However, thanks to companies like Amazon that eliminated the need to leave your couch to buy your goods, these retail stores were at risk of irrelevance. Gruenewald knew this. But where most (at this point in time) had seen this shift in the market as a **roadblock**, he saw the **opportunity** diamond in the rough. So when he approached the publishing behemoth Thomas Nelson, he presented a solution which would not only provide the Bible in a more accessible format than ever before but would simultaneously solve the publishing company's need for adapting to the shifting market conditions. Gruenewald convinced Thomas Nelson to consider their rights to the New International Version translation of the Bible as a "loss leader"[8] in exchange for direct access to the emails of the future Bible app

---

7 Coleman. Interview with Bobby Gruenewald.
8 Coleman. Interview with Bobby Gruenewald.

users.

While risky, the decision to say yes was probably the best decision Thomas Nelson could have made in order to stay both relevant and profitable. However, it didn't appear that way at first.

In 2007, the YouVersion website was launched, and the world was introduced to the first online version of the Bible. Yet despite the excitement about this achievment, nothing happened. Plenty of people visited the website, but it was clear that there was not much public interest in the product. (You know a product is a flop when not even its creators want to use it.) While they had set out with the intention of putting the Bible on a more mobile and portable platform than the paper books that had always been used, they inevitably discovered that desktop and laptop computers carried with them the same physical inconveniences as their analogue counterparts, if not more.

> *"If you had more resources you would just buy a solution. You wouldn't need to innovate."*
> - Bobby Gruenewald

Discouraged but not defeated, the team analyzed their failure and searched for where they went wrong. That's when they reached into their pant pockets and felt their blackberry phone. If you're too young to know what that is, think of a flip phone that posed as a smart phone, bragged about not needing an antenae since last week, and, oh yeah, it's got a whopping 2 megapixels of fun packed into its camera. (For perspective, the iPhone XS has 12 megapixels.) As antiquated as it may seem to us now, in 2007 it was an extremely viable solution.

That's when Apple announced the release of the

iPhone. This new product changed everything, especially when the creation of the Apple's App Store followed close behind in 2008. When Gruenewald first discovered this upcoming, exclusive source of apps for all of the countless iphones that were bound to be purchased in the near future, he knew he found his platform. So without adieu and with the help of a tech-savvy nineteen-year-old, he immediately launched into the creation of the Bible app. It was a simple app with no bells or whistles, just the Bible. And lo and behold, when the app store went live on July 10th of that year, YouVersion was one of the 200 apps first offered on Apple's exclusive platform. While Gruenewald admits to estimating between 50,000-60,000 downloads in the first year, his reasonable expectations were blown out of the water when 83,000 people downloaded the app in the very first weekend. Since then, more than 340 million people have downloaded it. It is now downloaded in every single country in 1,627 versions representing 1,169 languages.[9]

YouVersion faced numerous hurdles in becoming the leading Bible app in the dawn of a commercial and intellectual revolution, yet not one of these hurdles was absent from helping form the solution. Both their embrace of constraints and the speed in which they did so were critical factors in how they succeeded in innovating the way the world absorbs the Bible.

Explore, then Commit
Pickles and Ice Cream
If we return to the white sandy beach where our ex-

---

9 Coleman. Interview with Bobby Gruenewald.

plorer Will was last left in hopeless limbo, we can begin to explore just how important "zooming out" is in our quest for innovative solutions to social impact problems. Will had obviously learned the value of planning and executing courses of action before, having learned from his previously self-proclaimed reckless and impatient ways. You might say he was really good at taking clear, well-lit photos of the tree from six feet away. He knew the trunk and roots well and perhaps had a vague idea of what the branches most likely did as they extended outward and upward from the trunk, yet he was completely unaware of how the tree interacted within the larger sphere of its environment, being unable to see the forest for the trees.

How many times have design solutions failed because their process included taking a previous system or concept deemed inadequate for solving the current problem and tacking on new solid and viable idea(s), only to discover their Frankenstein is more horrifying monster than helpful man? Starting with pre-existing systems that have worked well in the past and adding on new ideas without reconsidering the system as a whole is like a **pickle ice cream sundae**: two good things mixed together do not always equal a better product.

If one seeks to resolve the core of a **need** instead of addressing the **problem** with its ingrained specks and flakes of preconceived notions of what the solution might be, one must effectively wipe the slate clean in order to look at the world with new eyes. In other words, one must **explore** before **committing** to an idea.

Empty Your Cup

The great martial arts legend Bruce Lee once told a story passed down from his instructor. A Japanese Zen master was visited by a college professor who claimed he desired to learn from the master. However, it soon became clear to the master that he merely wished to impress him with his knowledge of Zen. Upon seeing the professor's lack of interest to learn, the master suggested they have tea. As he poured the professor's tea, he intentionally continued filing the cup even after it started spilling over. When he could stand it no longer, the professor stated, "The cup is overfull, no more will go in." The master nodded and said, "Like this cup you are full of your own opinions and speculations. How can I show you Zen unless you first empty your cup?"[10]

The Skateboard

One of my biggest challenges as a designer has always been the ability to simplify my design. Too often throughout my design process I discover numerous good ideas that, by themselves, seem quite excellent.

---

10 Hyams. *Zen in the Martial Arts*.

Yet as the process progresses, I discover that the original concept is no longer sufficient based upon realizations gathered from further exploration. Instead of pursuing a holistic solution that organically arises out of a clear understanding of all applicable data, I, like the self-confident professor, take the lazy approach, choosing to keep my now stalled-out idea and adding other intrinsically insightful yet extrinsically inappropriate concepts. This results in what I can only refer to as a "Frankensteinian" (Google says that's a word) end result.

To give another more modern car example of innovation, we need look no further than to Tesla's revolutionary Model S design. While electric cars have existed since the 19th century, after 1920 they were never given much credence due to lack of engineering and economical market viability.[11] So, it was instead the gas-powered vehicle that received all of the attention over the coming century, becoming more efficient, faster, and sleeker. The electric car would occasionally poke its head in on the technology innovation conversation, only to continually be laughed out of the room time and time again (sound familiar?).

Due to its lack of available funding, electric car visionaries were left looking at the problem from six feet away, leaving the gas-free piece of engineering far from the adjacent possible. In order to simplify the design process, engineers chose to analyze the problem through a lens of substitution rather than reinvention. In order to handle the different power source (a bunch of bulky batteries and not a tank of liquid gas), the easiest and most direct solution seemed to be to place the batteries somewhere in the vehicle, such as the trunk. For the longest time, this substitutional approach dominated the discussion of development, prohibiting the

---

11 Matulka. "Timeline."

industry from ever accomplishing any real progress in the matter.[12]

Enter Tesla.

Having basically written the book on innovation, Tesla CEO Elon Musk chose a different path for his work. Instead of the substitution approach, he stepped back to look at the problem from a sixty-foot view. In stepping back, Musk took note of the then isolated occurrence of innovative lithium ion battery development, seeing the perfect opportunity to piggyback these advances in battery technology with his own engineering endeavors. Doing such research for the sole application of his electric vehicle would have been too expensive to conduct by himself, whereas his tandem approach toward innovation created a platform from which a point of view was generated that had never before existed.

The result was a skateboard.[13]

That's what Tesla called their innovative new chassis system, completely redesigned from the ground up. Instead of thinking of the motor, suspension, and power source as all separate components—as the gas-powered vehicle had done for so many years—Tesla realized that within the realm of possibility created by the development in lithium ion battery technology lie the possibility for something amazing. If you imagine how a typical gas-powered vehicle goes together with a rigid metal frame that supports a motor in the front that separately powers the front and rear axles connected by a long drive shaft, all of which lies clumsily underneath the cabin, you can see it's a lot of parts and pieces.

Now image a skateboard, a relatively flat low-profile surface, with two motors that separately power the front and the back wheels and upon which the main

---

12 Matulka. "Timeline."
13 Simpson. "The Tesla Model S."

cabin of the car rests. Yet this skateboard motif was only made possible due to the advancement in lithium ion battery technology as these batteries were now able to be distributed equally along the rigid platform at the bottom of the vehicle, the "skateboard." Not only is its slim profile more aerodynamic than its counterpart, it's also safer, more human friendly (no more obnoxious hump created from the drive shaft on the floor for the poor child forced to sit in the middle), and more spacious.[14]

It's a broad stroke overview, but do you get the picture? By stepping back and allowing himself the freedom to explore seemingly unrelated advancements such as lithium ion batteries, Musk was able to commit to a solution that never would have been possible if he had stuck with the pre-existing conditions. Author and journalist Charles Duhigg calls these types of people "innovation brokers," describing them as "the people most skilled at taking existing information, answers, and resources, and applying them as solutions to new problems."[15] As an innovation broker, Musk had the ability and insight to "import" ideas from one realm and give them new life by bringing them into a different one.

Straddling
The lesson of Explore, then Commit, is two-fold. While it is important not to commit to yesterday's idea before exploring what tomorrow will bring, it is equally important that one, upon sufficient exploration, commit to their direction instead of pursuing multiple design directions much like my early design days. The term "straddling" succinctly describes the problem of trying to chase two rabbits and effectively catching none. If

---

14 Simpson
15 Coleman. Interview with Charles Duhigg.

you are unable to choose between two options, instead choosing to "straddle" both, you won't get very far. It's like trying to ride two horses at the same time; it gets sketchy when they decide to go different directions.

Eclecticism

This is not to say that we should discount the value of exploration and eclecticism in design. By definition, eclecticism draws upon "multiple theories, styles, or ideas to gain complementary insights into a subject."[16] This is a wonderful approach and is the clear praxis of the Zen principle I applied earlier of emptying one's cup. In fact, eclecticism, in following the martial arts analogy, is now considered an inherent component of nearly all development in the martial arts. As a martial arts teacher myself, I have spent years adding experience, training, and insight into my own American Karate curriculum, inserting numerous components from other styles

---

16 New World Encyclopedia, s.v. "eclecticism," accessed 2018. http://www.newworldencyclopedia.org/entry/Eclecticism.

such as Kenpo, Brazilian Jiu-Jitsu, and the Keysi Fighting Method. Yet before I would insert any new movements or ideas into my own system, I always ensured that said movement or idea adhered to the values and beliefs I held to be integral to my teaching.

When standing farther and farther away from the design problem, the number of available solution contributions can seem to grow exponentially, creating a mound of possible solutions. Don't let this wear you down. One of the beautiful aspects of the sixty-foot view (or ideation phase, as it is often called) is best summarized by "the spaghetti phase." The spaghetti phase is the limited period of time in which one is free to take all of the wet noodles of ideas that you have, launch them against the wall, and then see what sticks. Take advantage of the opportunity to explore multiple ideas, thoughts, and possibilities.

A very practical example of this spaghetti-throwing frenzy is cross-industry innovation. In regards to the importance of cross-industry innovation in business, Research Fellow Bart Devoldere says this:

> Disruptive new business models, like that of Airbnb, do not stem from the traditional hotel industry. In the case of Airbnb, it is the digital industry which is having an extremely unsettling impact on various industries. But whereas benchmarking only draws a comparison between you and your competitors, cross-industry innovation can offer a more unique and creative approach which will allow you to differentiate in the longer term.[17]

This cross-industry innovation not only acts as an idea generator, it also provides insight into previously un-

---

17 Devoldere. "The Importance of Cross-Industry Innovation."

foreseen partnership possibilities. Devoldere continues:

> Ultimately, the essence of every company boils down to the same thing: you offer a solution to a problem. Someone has a problem or a demand and you provide a solution. If you know which problems your business solves and dig deeper, you can take a broader view to see which other industries, even those far removed from your own line of business, are also engaged in solving this problem.[18]

As in every industry, those who are innovating (and succeeding) in SID are more often than not the ones who are looking at players across the seemingly unrelated field to figure out their game.

Cross-industry innovation is eclecticism at its core since it entails the pursuit of creative solutions regardless of their source. In order to successfully innovate the formation of your social impact organization, eclecticism should likely be an integral component of your exploration. Only once you have emptied your cup and explored the unknown should you claim your lane and commit to your direction. Once you have committed, the key to maintaining clarity and avoiding the "straddling" conundrum is the holistic synthesis of all the raw ingredients, resulting in one fixed solution driven by a **logical** and **holistic** set of guidelines rather than a confusing conglomeration of disjointed entities.

In other words, either eat a pickle or enjoy a sundae.

---

18 Devoldere

A-Ha!

When 100 Fold Studio founder John Hudson began exploring the realm of possibilities for what his innovative design firm could be, he intentionally took a step back before committing to an idea, choosing instead to seek inspiration from non-typical sources. John claims his "A-Ha!" moment came when he began exploring the story behind the founding of Habitat for Humanity. The non-profit organization currently exists to help those in need build or improve the place they call home, but that wasn't always its purpose. In fact, it was originally founded by a lawyer in Alabama seeking to help provide affordable mortgages to people in need.[19] This pivot of direction that Habitat took to accomplish its goal through unexpected mediums challenged Hudson to do the same.

Now, after similar iterations of rediscovery and big-picture thinking, 100 Fold Studio has emerged rebranded no longer as "an architecture firm that happens to train" but rather "a training studio that happens to do architecture."[20] We will discuss this more in Chapter 6, but suffice it to say that looking beyond the industry standard practice of non-profit architecture firms was what propelled 100 Fold Studio along their own unique journey of SID.

Sick Buildings

A tangible, more project-based example of how Frankenstein was avoided can be found across the Atlantic Ocean in the Rwandan city of Kigali. International architecture firm MASS Design Group had been hired by the Partners In Health (PIH) in 2007 to help plan and design a state-of-the-art hospital facility (the first in its district)

---

19 John Hudson (Founder, 100 Fold Studio), interviewed by Jacob DeNeui in Battambang, Cambodia, July 14, 2017.
20 John Hudson

that would help create a healing environment for the people of the Butaro District.[21] What resulted was a holistic design that helped mitigate and reduce transmission of airborne disease through innovative systems, including the maximization of natural ventilation.

    To some, this may not seem very innovative. Rather, it may actually appear to be the opposite of innovative. Wouldn't the absence of highly advanced mechanical systems and construction systems designed to forcefully mitigate the threat of airborne diseases be inherently less innovative, a step backward in the pursuit of greater, more effective technology?

    Not if you understood the situation from the sixty-foot point of view.

    Years before MASS would partner with PIH, co-founder Michael Murphy attended a lecture by Dr. Paul Farmer, one of the co-founders of PIH. At the lecture, Murphy learned that in South Africa, certain buildings were actually making people sicker. Certain western construction systems had made their way into the building practices of the area that essentially made the buildings more airtight. However, unlike most western buildings, the hallways in the treatment center were left unventilated, most likely due to economic restrictions. What resulted was a patient entering with a broken arm and leaving with a multi-drug resistant strain of tuberculosis.[22]

    It appeared that buildings were making people sicker.

> *"The mark of a designer is a willing embrace of constraints."*
>   - Charles Eames

---

21 TED. "Architecture That's Built to Heal."
22 TED

    Instead of solving the problem through western-style methodologies, Murphy chose to step back in order to develop a holistic solution that addressed the true problem through available means. The design team began to look at utilizing passive ventilation strategies that didn't require mechanical systems. (Previous attempts to insert such systems seemed to inevitably fail due to a number of reasons, not the least being the inability to maintain such systems.) By stepping away from the tree, they were able to more fully comprehend what would be required for success for the project. Often, the success of a design can be interpolated from the level of a designer's awareness and embrace of design constraints embedded in the situation. Designer Charles Eames agreed with Mr. Gruenewald when he said "the mark of a designer is a willing embrace of constraints."[23]

    Had MASS not willingly embraced the constraints of this project, instead choosing to design around westernized mechanical solutions for disease prevention, the lack of available maintenance in Kigali would probably have turned the HVAC units into giant mold dispensers throughout the whole building. Talk about a pickle ice cream sundae!

23 Brown

Adapt or Die

Before we wrap up our discussion on these three design tools, let's take another look at the story of Blockbuster. In 2000, Blockbuster and Netflix came head to head in a decisive battle of strategy when Netflix founder Reed Hastings proposed a partnership to Blockbuster CEO John Antioco and his team. Hastings's offer was rejected, not because the Blockbuster team thought Hastings's idea was bad but rather because they thought they could still compete.[24]

And Blockbuster did indeed try to compete.

Forbes contributor Greg Satell states, "The irony is that Blockbuster failed because its leadership had built a well-oiled operational machine. It was a very tight network that could execute with extreme efficiency, but poorly suited to let in new information."[25] Saving the ship would take more than the minor addition of a new subscription policy as a revenue stream to an already grounded and solidified company that had built a large portion of its profit margins around the idea of late fees.

To experience the benefits of effective innovation, social impact entrepreneurs must first separate the problem from ill-informed ideas they might have regarding its solution, embrace constraints as opportunities, and become well-suited to let in new information. Choosing to simply add to existing approaches while avoiding roadblocks or "emptying your cup" might seem like the safe choice. It will possibly bring you cautiously and prudently to the sandy beach you thought you wanted to get to, only to find that you had cautiously and prudently set off in the wrong direction. Identify your self-damaging biases. Embrace the opportunity

24 Satell. "A Look Back."
25 Satell

roadblocks represent. Don't fear the exploration of eclectic ideas during your spaghetti phase.

Mosaics

In the final three chapters, we will focus our discussion on three channels of innovation that are particularly relevant in today's age. Through this, we will learn how differentiating between the need and the problem has contributed greatly to current innovative solutions. The beauty of this process is that, while operating in realms of seemingly uncreative topics like purpose, funding, and resources, there is tremendous potential for creativity within these pursuits. In fact, it is vital that one utilizes the same creativity for designing their **METHOD** as designers would use for designing their **PRODUCT**. Each and every one of us is a unique and priceless mosaic of experiences, insights, and abilities that come together in a creative collage to form the perfect tool for designing your organization. Internationally renowned drummer Zoro (aka the "Minister of Groove") put it best when he said, "your uniqueness will shape your innovation."[26] The extent to which you harness your uniqueness will be the cap upon your effectiveness.

> *The extent to which you harness your uniqueness will be the cap upon your effectiveness.*

Step back so you can see the forest for the trees. Otherwise, you may end up with a pickle ice cream sundae.

---

26 Coleman, Ken. Interview with Zoro the Drummer.

Chapter 5 in a page...

- Designers must address the **problem** instead of the **need** or they'll inevitably "taint" their solution with the addition of ill-informed preconceived notions.
- Seeking to understand the issue from multiple points of view will help one arrive at a less biased understanding of the problem.
- Roadblocks in the design process will prompt **destruction**, **apathy**, or **innovation**.
- Even the most undesired **roadblocks** (i.e., blindness) can be taken advantage of and turned into **opportunities**.
- If you're looking for a strategic partnership, try to find a mutually beneficial solution to a problem you are both experiencing.
- **Empty your cup** in order to **explore** multiple ideas and industries to increase your chances of discovering an **eclectic** solution that may never have been thought of before.
- Once you've landed on a direction that appears to hold promise, **commit** to it and say no to Frankenstein.

Food for Thought...

1. Find someone in your field who tends to see things in life from a different point of view and ask them what they see as the greatest problem(s) your industry faces today.
2. Think back to some of the times your plans/ideas were interrupted by a challenge. Did you treat it as roadblock or an opportunity? If a roadblock, how could you have viewed it as a constructive constraint?
3. Find two to three podcasts, magazines, or any form of information that are completely unrelated to your field and see what you can learn from them. Then, consider making that cross-industry exploration a part of your routine.

Chapter 6

YOU DO YOU, BOO

"One day Alice came to a fork in the road and saw a Cheshire cat in a tree. 'Which road do I take?' she asked. 'Where do you want to go?' was his response. 'I don't know' Alice answered. 'Then,' said the cat, 'it doesn't matter.'"
- Alice in Wonderland

Design Twister
Life is a journey, isn't it? One moment the wind is gustily propelling you forward, the road ahead is bright and full of opportunities every which way you look, and then in an instant everything changes. The path you thought you were on does an about-face, and soon up is down, left is right, and country music is pop with a twang. Life sometimes seems to throw more curveballs than the World Series. While many of life's players tend to prefer the slow, predictable underhand serve, designers (social entrepreneurs included), of all people, have a particular affinity for the messy, colorful kaleidoscope of options that we are given every day. In fact, the most innovative designers are the ones who pursue the mess for the purpose of creating something that leaves the world breathless.

Designer Bjarke Ingels, known as one of the world's currently most innovative architects, believes in the idea that to achieve what design has never achieved before, one must explore what has never been explored. He uses the awkwardly humorous example of an "architectural game of twister."¹ In case you've never played Twister before, I guarantee you'll see and experience things you never would have seen or experienced before playing that round (some things you might wish you could unsee). In Ingels's example, "You start in a traditional pose, and then as you pile on demands, suddenly you find yourself in a back bend with your face rubbing up against the private parts of your family members, and it becomes enjoyable and fun."² Think about that for a second—laugh—now dismiss it forever.

Ingels's use of body manipulation is a brilliant form of illustrating what the process of designing your purpose should look like. In this early, explorative stage of forming your social impact organization, it is often essential to transition from the "traditional pose" as we twist, bend, and mold our viewpoint and perspective in order to see the world from a different point of view. It is only when we choose to open up the spice cabinet instead of instinctually reaching for the salt shaker that we begin to explore the aromatic and tantalizing possibilities of what could be.

> *The most innovative designers are the ones who pursue the mess for the purpose of creating something that leaves the world breathless.*

---

1 The New York Times Conferences. "Infrastructure with Bjarke Ingels."
2 The New York Times Conferences.

Kill Your Darlings

Laying aside the food analogy for a bit (you'll soon understand why), I'm reminded of the compelling story of architect-turned-sewer-designer Julia King. After receiving a full scholarship by the London Metropolitan University to pursue her Ph.D-by-practice, King travelled south to the fringes of Delhi, a slum resettlement colony called Savda Ghevra, in order to help alleviate the residents there of their poverty through architectural intervention.

That's when she realized she was wrong.

After she began to immerse herself in the local culture, King began to understand that the community around her was fully capable of designing and building their residences. The "problem" was sanitary sewage, not a need for better schools or homes. King states, "I remember thinking I am going to come and build houses but I very quickly realized that if you want to build houses you have to build sewers first. So, my inspiration never so much came from me—it came from the site."[3]

Stephen King gave us some brutally helpful advice when he said this: "Kill your darlings, kill your darlings, even when it breaks your egocentric little …

---

3 Quirk. "Introducing 'Potty-Girl'."

heart, kill your darlings."[4] I have no doubt that Julia King would have done a fine job at designing impactful and inspiring houses for the Indian community she chose to serve. Likely, they would have been safe and inspiring, like having one foot on blue and one foot on yellow (if you have no idea what I mean, put the book down and go play Twister). However, something far greater and more impactful awaited the people of Savda Ghevra through King's creativity and her desire to transform lives. This was no doubt difficult for King, at least at first. Designing sewage transportation is far less glamorous than designing houses, yet King's willingness to sacrifice glamour for impact is exactly what makes her story so compelling. She was forced to choose between cuddling with her darling idea of designing houses in India or killing it in order to embrace a new idea that aligned with the realities of Savda Ghevra's needs. Clearly, King knew how to see past the need into the problem. Her strategic abilities to observe, diagnose, and treat the actual root of the problem through her unique design capabilities clearly demonstrate the essence of this chapter: achieving lasting impact that supersedes your narrow understanding of what your clients need requires intentional design of your purpose, no matter what the cost.

4 King. *On Writing*.

Sid understood the heart of this message quite well. While Peter operated under the paradigm that his purpose was simply to do something, and Will with the understanding that his purpose was to get to the east coast, Sid knew something the first two missed: a broken understanding of one's purpose produces broken results.

A humorous example of this is the work of one graduate student in his clinical study of aiding alcoholics on their road to recovery. Working with renowned psychologist Albert Bandura, the student formulated the hypothesis that, due to the fact that many alcoholics stuffer from tremendous stress, it would be advantageous to provide tools for these alcoholics to practice relaxation in order to overcome their stress. It turns out the alcoholics proved to be excellent at the art of relaxing, resulting in a room full of not recovered yet completely relaxed drunks.[5]

A broken understanding of one's purpose produces broken results

Mushrooms and Failure

We may laugh at the irony of this situation yet, humorous as it is, it demonstrates an excellent point. Science and design share a close bond as they both require an initial curiosity, a process of observation and exploration, and creation and refinement of a hypothesis (exploration before commitment). It is important to understand ahead of time that there may be (and likely will be) times when a proposed hypothesis turns out to be wrong. This is true of the majority of all scientific findings and hypotheses. Creating a proposal for your social

---

5 Patterson. *Influencer.*

impact venture and later discovering that it was not the best direction is not inherently a failure, but rather it might simply be confirmation that you are on the right track. I have chosen to make it a practice to observe the conditions of my failures, recognize the lessons learned, and continue on knowing I'm better for it. Winston Churchill is credited with saying that "success consists of going from failure to failure without loss of enthusiasm," so in designing your purpose, I would encourage you to embrace failure as a sign of healthy innovation and an entrepreneurial spirit.

The key in this embrace of failure is to recognize and distinguish the difference between good failure and bad failure. Good failure is when you follow the sound practices of scientific exploration yet still do not produce the desired results. Bad failure is caused by a lack of adherence to logical steps of exploration and development. In other words, good failure is the starving man who dies from biting into the unknown yet poisonous mushroom. Bad failure is the friend who finishes the mushroom for him.

A Fortuitous Relationship
John Hudson, founder of the international non-profit architecture firm 100 Fold Studio, is a mushroom eater. Hudson started 100 Fold Studio with no experience running an international non-profit but simply a healthy level of innovativeness and a solid foundation of experience in the for-profit realm. While Hudson did extensive research into the field he was about to enter (see Chapter 5), there was no singular source with all of the answers for how to run his organization (the thing about innovation is that nobody has ever done it exactly that way before), so he continued blazing his own trail in this brave new world he had entered.

In 2010, 100 Fold Studio was launched. It began with small projects, primarily for the non-profit organization Youth With a Mission (YWAM) that it had partnered with, including a small campus master plan, deck remodels, and building cladding upgrades. While beneficial and appreciated, after several years and only six built projects, the firm's success seemed to be slow in coming.

That is until Hudson stopped to **design** the **purpose** of 100 Fold Studio.

Since the beginning, 100 Fold Studio had focused primarily on architectural design (Hudson was, after all, an architect). His experience with owning his own firm made him a very qualified architectural designer and professional. What was missing, however, was something that 100 Fold Studio had been doing all along but had yet to be capitalized upon. "We're discovering that how you do business is the cool thing. We just happen to do architecture, but we're really a training organization,"[6] says Hudson. Beginning in 2011, 100 Fold Studio had begun what would eventually become its legacy: training young social impact designers who believed architecture could transform lives by transforming spaces. In the summer of 2011, 100 Fold Studio began investing in the lives of a handful of young college students with its first summer

> *Good failure is the starving man who dies from biting into the unknown yet poisonous mushroom. Bad failure is the friend who finishes the mushroom for him.*

---

6 John Hudson (Founder, 100 Fold Studio), interviewed by Jacob deNeui in Battambang, Cambodia, July 14, 2017.

internships, accepting six young designers and administrative professionals into their "fold" and providing them first-hand experience of what architectural design in an international non-profit firm could look like.

One of those designers was me.

To this day I still remember the night I discovered 100 Fold Studio. It had been a long but exciting day in San Diego at the Spring West Quad Conference, a biannual conference put on by the American Institute of Architecture Students (AIAS). After an evening of festivities, my introverted angel had finally convinced me to retreat to my hotel room and work on my design project so as not to fall too far behind when I returned to school the next week. Upon needing a brain break, my eyes shifted to my email to temporarily divert my attention. One subject line in particular caught my eye, so I opened it to read more about this summer internship. In no time at all, I knew it would be the opportunity of a lifetime. I'm not lying when I say that my resume and portfolio were emailed to the address given within minutes of finishing that email. The rest, as they say, is history. To say my two months with 100 Fold Studio were transformative would be an understatement. Since that summer, the firm has hosted more than 60 young design professionals in their summer program. (It has since been named Summer Studio.)

However, this clarity about their purpose was not born right away. The spark that would ignite this flame in 100 Fold Studio's journey would present itself years later in the form of a fortuitous relationship with a community and education-oriented venture group called Praxis Labs, a non-profit organization focused on creating cultural and social impact through entrepreneurship. After 100 Fold Studio was accepted into one of Praxis's accelerator programs, Hudson was able to pull from their collective perspectives and wisdom in order to redirect the focus of the organization. "We kind of fumbled into it. Praxis helped us clarify who we are,"[7] he says, though fumble might be too humble of a term. Due to 100 Fold Studio's intentional and deliberate approach to designing their vision for creating lasting change in the world, the epiphany they received through the guidance of Praxis was simply the logical next step. Hudson adds, "The delivery method is what amazes us now. It's the training that's actually going to be more beneficial than the charity."[8] By incorporating the flexibility necessary to approach their purpose from all different angles into their formation process, 100 Fold Studio was able to successfully realize where their innate strengths were and how that then positioned them for success. In other words, they looked at the tree from multiple points of view.

7 John Hudson
8 John Hudson

All about Who You Know

100 Fold Studio is but one of multiple SID organizations that have innovated in their approach to discovering their unique purpose. Architecture for Humanity (AFH), one of the most well-known SID organizations of the past two decades, served as a shining example of how to capitalize upon your strengths in pursuing change in the world. AFH was started in 1999 by co-founders Cameron Sinclair and Kate Stohr in an effort to empower designers who were tired of waiting to create change in the world. At that time, war in Kosovo was ravaging the people of that nation, leaving roughly 12,000 dead and countless without shelter. Sinclair and Stohr both felt powerfully moved to do something about the travesty, which led to the birth of AFH. Instead of simply designing a possible solution for the crisis themselves, Sinclair and Stohr created a website and launched an international design competition in order to maximize both the awareness of the crisis as well as the number of proposed design solutions.[9]

The results were staggering.

Hundreds of entries poured into their emails from around the world. AFH had found its **purpose**. In reference to his atypical application of his architectural training, Sinclair states, "My role is not as a designer; it's as a **conduit** between the design world and the humanitarian world."[10] Sinclair knew that achieving the results he found aggravatingly absent from the design world would require an entirely different and innovative approach to how he utilized his particular skill set and passions. By 2004, AFH had grown bigger than Stohr and Sinclair knew how to handle, which led to the next phase in AFH's growth. "I really couldn't man-

---

9 Sinclair. "My Wish."
10 Sinclair

age the number of people who wanted to help, or the number of requests that I was getting. So, we decided to embrace an open-source model of business—so that anyone, anywhere in the world, could start a local chapter, and they can get involved in local problems."[11] While certainly a new platform, Sinclair still saw his and AFH's purpose as that of a **connector**, a social link supporting designers from across the world in their goal of using design to solve big humanitarian needs that, in their view, were currently being left unaddressed. "This isn't just about non-profit. There's a grassroots movement going on, of socially responsible designers who really believe that this world has got a lot smaller, and that we have the opportunity—not the responsibility, but the opportunity—to really get involved in making change."[12]

SID Grows Up

Unfortunately, AFH was forced to close its doors in 2015. However, their legacy as a beacon of innovation and force for social change through design still lives on, particularly through the relatively recent emergence of its offshoot organization Open Architecture Collaborative (OAC) in 2016. Founder Garrett Jacobs, a previous employee at AFH, states, "It's a whole different organizational structure. It's more of an educational organization with huge component of community organizing and amplification of the work that's on the ground."[13] Due to the strong remaining network of individual AFH chapters left after the mothership dissolved, OAC was able to rise from the ashes as a "substitutionary" phoenix of sorts. Jacobs claims that it was through the trial and error method of AFH's bold innovation and experimen-

---

11 Sinclair
12 Sinclair
13 Taylor-Hochberg. Interview with Garrett Jacobs.

tation that OAC was able to organize itself as more of a project **support** resource rather than the actual executor of the project.

Innovation Tension
Now comes the curve ball. The great value of OAC and AFH's role in the story of SID is the important lesson it teaches about the continual need for innovation BALANCED with the need for stability. Allow me to explain. Since AFH's conception, their original organization model has grown in popularity and acceptance. Other organizations such as OAC and 100 Fold Studio have since then built upon the foundation that AFH laid while tweaking and innovating along the way. Standing upon the shoulders of giants is the only way in which we will ever create a field where social impact organizations are both common and sustainable, and this end goal is not insignificant.

One way to identify a mature and healthy field of work is to see if it is or is not occupied primarily by innovators (not that the presence of any innovators would inherently indicate immaturity). However, social entrepreneurs—specifically social impact designers—have steep challenges before them as they strive to influence a field that is still relatively fresh. Designer and researcher Mia Scharpie claims that until SID is no longer filled with only innovators but begins to develop a "rank and file" population, it will fail to grow into maturity, stating, "a field that is filled with people who are just innovators and entrepreneurs is not a mature field."[14]

Eric Ries, author of *The Lean Startup*, would agree. Ries points to the disadvantage that industry underdogs have when it comes to creating progress in their area of expertise, stating that "planning and forecasting are only

14 Interview with Mia Scharpie

accurate when based on a long, stable operating history and a relatively static environment. Startups have neither."[15] By continually building upon the foundations set by other innovators, whether in the past or the present, social entrepreneurs will continue to grow and mature their fields as a whole in their efforts to provide services that respect the dignity and worth of all mankind.

It is important to point out how easy it is to confuse **innovation** with the actual goal of **effectiveness**. This misunderstanding would easily lead one to pursue innovation purely for the sake of innovation. Yet as Scharpie and Ries pointed out, seeking only innovation would neglect the value and importance of the stability and strength that result from the evolution of innovation into standard practices. Building upon the analogy that "design is like the railroad tracks that guide and enable the engine of innovation," effectiveness is the destination at which the engine of innovation should arrive.

I stated in the Introduction that our exploration of SID will demonstrate how the presence of controlled amounts of innovation is connected to that field's effectiveness. Essentially what it comes down to is a dichotomy of pursuing both continual innovation while simultaneously pursuing the "static environment,"[16] as Ries put it, that accompanies stable fields. Both of these are accomplished when social entrepreneurs pursue **effectiveness** in their cause by applying **innovative design thinking** in their formation. Each and every time a social impact entrepreneur innovates his or her purpose, it provides a fresh perspective on the field and eventually, a possible case study which may then be utilized by future innovators as they design their own endeavors.

15 Ries. *The Lean Startup.*
16 Ries

Pro Bono

John Cary, founder of Impact Design Hub (IDH), a non-profit organization whose focus is to be "a resource for designing a better world"[17] serves as another example of innovating your purpose. In essence, IDH operates with the clear purpose of providing primarily informational **resources** for social impact designers out there through the form of written content, connection to outside tools and opportunities, and their podcast *The Fun Palace*. It's a very clear and unique direction IDH has taken, and similar to OAC, IDH had some mighty fine giant shoulders to stand upon. Before embarking upon the creation of IDH, founder Jon Cary was involved with another organization called Public Architecture. Cary was the organization's first full-time employee after founder John Peterson began the organization in 2002 with what he refers to as "unbridled enthusiasm and convenient naivety."[18] Peterson founded Public Architecture to "show firms that pro bono* service is good for business, and [to] help the non-profit and philanthropic sectors understand the valuable role that design can play in advancing their causes."[19] Cary adds that "Public Architecture's real legacy is the intense interest and passion for pro bono service in the design community and non-profit world."[20]

> *Effectiveness is the destination at which the engine of innovation should arrive.*

   Public Architecture was dissatisfied with the

---

17 Cary. *The Power of Pro Bono*.
18 Peterson. "Public Architecture."
19 Cary
20 Cary

minimal amount of involvement in pro bono work that the mainstream architecture industry was known for. Pro bono is short for the Latin phrase *pro bono publico,* meaning "for the public good,"[21] not "for free" as many have come to understand it. The rectification of this misunderstanding of the term is a passion of John Peterson's and served as a primary motivator for the formation of Public Architecture. In seeking out successful enactors of the true pro bono ideology, Public Architecture looked to the example of the legal profession in particular due to their noteworthy championing of the pro bono ideology. The practice of pro bono is even explicitly condoned within the bylaws of the American Bar Association as well as the individual state entities responsible for licensing attorneys. In fact, the legal profession is quite well known for charity, giving on average 2.5 percent of their fees toward pro bono work, two and a half times the accepted corporate standard of 1 percent.[22]

With this wind in their sails, Public Architecture proceeded to create what is now known as 1+, an initiative that rallies the architectural industry to join together in donating 1 percent or more of its design services toward public good. This essentially comes down to each designer donating twenty hours of work each year. 1+ not only seeks to increase the quantity of donated services but also the quality. As of 2010, the program had helped to bring together over 750 firms in donating over 250,000 hours of their services, or essentially $25 million of donated services annually.[23]

In essence, Public Architecture designed its pur-

---

21 Collins Dictionary, s.v. "pro bono publico," accessed 2018. https://www.collinsdictionary.com/us/dictionary/english/pro-bono-publico.
22 Cary
23 Cary

pose around the idea of advocacy.

No Man Is an Island
What is it, then, that connects all of these social impact design initiatives besides their varying level of connection to the architectural field? Remember that, while they are all either directly or indirectly involved in the creation of SID, none of them operate strictly within the role of what would be considered a traditional architectural designer. Instead, each of these organizations channeled their unique gifts and passions through the lens of innovation, creating the following innovative purposes for their organization:

- **TRAINING –** 100 Fold Studio transitioned from "an architecture firm that happens to train" to "a training organization that happens to do architecture."
- **CONNECTION –** Architecture for Humanity and Open Architecture Collaborative discovered the greatest use of its resources was to connect designers with opportunities.
- **ADVOCACY –** Public Architecture channeled its passion for pro bono work within architecture by advocating for firms to donate 1 percent of their services to pro bono work.
- **EQUIPPING –** Impact Design Hub, Public Architecture's brain child of sorts, found its place as a database of resources for social impact designers.

While these one-word labels do far from justice in describing the unique missions of these organizations, this categorization is meant to illustrate how each one has found a way to innovate within their field by designing their purpose. As it is said, no man is an island. In the same way, each of these endeavors was built upon the explorations and achievements of those that went before them. Sometimes, alterations in structure or approach to social impact design stem from observed failures or perceived negative results while other times the reason may simply be a difference in desired trajectory based on preference, ideology, or skill set. Regardless of the reason, one can see the threads that tie all of these endeavors together as a unified whole, a kaleidoscope of brothers and sisters in arms with the unified goal of bringing positive change by respecting the dignity and value of all mankind.

    Creating lasting, noteworthy change within social impact fields is possible for any social entrepreneur, regardless of their previous experience, when starting at the very beginning stage of exploring purpose.

    Now that the topic of purpose has been addressed, we can begin exploring other components of innovation, beginning with that of funding, the topic of our next chapter of exploration.

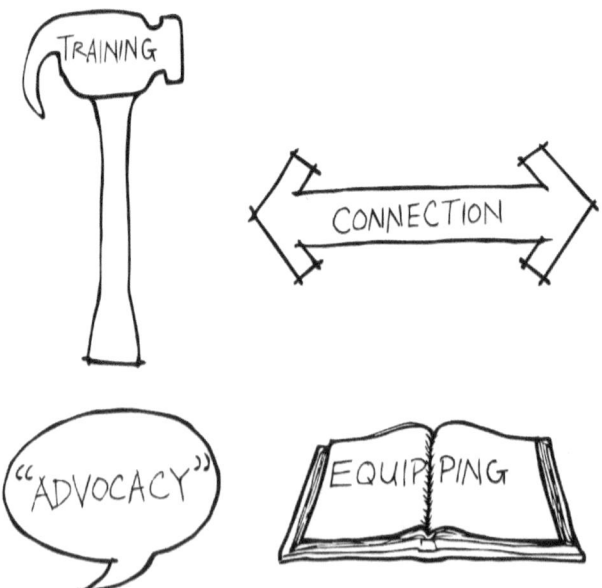

Chapter 6 in a page...

- Similar to a game of Twister, designing your purpose should entail a rich exploration from multiple points of views and positions.
- Be willing to kill your darlings. If your original concept of your purpose doesn't hold water, it's time for another cup.
- Success embraces good failures with undiminished enthusiasm, but not bad failures (i.e., don't finish the mushroom that killed your buddy).
- Innovation is the tool, but effectiveness is the goal; only once social impact fields have both industry stability and continual innovation will they be fully effective.
- Design your purpose as you discover your uniqueness, much like 100 Fold Studio, Architecture for Humanity, Public Architecture, and Impact Design Hub customized theirs.

Food for Thought...

1. Have you ever sat down and made your elevator pitch? Why do you exist? What do you do and how do you do it? Even if you have already, take a step back and brainstorm. Don't constrain yourself to normal ideas! Start crazy and see where you end up.
2. Are there "darlings" in your purpose statement that perhaps need to die? Try to objectively ask yourself if any part of your existing (or proposed) purpose needs to be replaced by something else.
3. What makes you unique? Ask yourself but also ask people who know you or your existing organization the best.

CASE STUDY
with Liz Forkin Bohannon

COMPANY TYPE	Private
YEAR FOUNDED	2009
LOCATION	Portland, OR
ESTIMATED REVENUE	$2.1 million
APPROXIMATE NUMBER OF EMPLOYEES	65[1]

Impact

I just bought a beautiful pair of brass earrings for my sister's Christmas gift. I don't know much about earrings (or any jewelry for that matter), but I know that they are shiny, they look pretty trendy, and they were handmade by a motivated girl in Uganda named Stella who is working to pay for her college education. Thanks to Sseko Designs (pronounced SAY-ko), Stella now has a shot at an education that was previously unavailable to her due to her gender and her country's economic depravity.

    Sseko Designs is an ethical fashion brand based in Uganda that creates beautiful handbags, accessories, and leather sandals with the express intent of equipping high-capacity Ugandan women with the ability to attend university. The company has been featured in numerous well-known publications including *Vogue, Redbook, Shape, Fitness, O Magazine, Fast Company, People*, and *Huffington Post*.

[1] "Sseko Design's Competitors"

The business model was created with the goal of "[solving] a non-profit problem with a for-profit solution" as founder and CEO Liz Forkin Bohannon put it.[2] Employees are picked exclusively from a pool of Ugandan women who have tested into college but simply can't afford to go. They are hired straight out of high school for the nine months between high school and the start of university—receiving a fair and equitable salary from their work, 50 percent of which is automatically rerouted to a savings account that employees can access once they reach university. Sseko will then match between 100–400 percent of that amount in the form of a university scholarship, all with the express purpose of overcoming financial and social inequality through means of a smart, high-quality business model. Over nine years, this model has granted over 100 Ugandan women the previously unimaginable privilege of graduating from university.

Story
"You don't have to go to another country to experience social injustice," says Bohannon in regards to how her social impact journey began in her home of St. Louis, Missouri. In 2012, St. Louis was reported to have a poverty rate of 29.3 percent, a nearly 2 percent increase from the previous year, and it's a fact that Bohannon attributes partially to her awareness of and heart for solving social injustice. Her mom's work as a pediatric nurse in a particularly poor section of St. Louis and habit of welcoming sick children into their home and family also helped shape her heart for the oppressed and afflicted, which is probably part of the reason why she attended the University of Missouri-Columbia to study journalism in order to be "the next Nick Kristof" (a *New York Times* reporter on issues regarding human rights, women's

[2]All direct quotes in this case study, as well as information about Sseko Designs, are from the following source: Kaufholz. Interview with Liz Forkin Bohannon.

rights, health, and global affairs).

However, after being armed with two master's degrees in both journalism and strategic communications, Bohannon was met with closed doors in her search for what she calls the "classic millennial" pursuit of a job that would allow her to follow all her passions, get paid, and top it all off with health insurance—forcing her to take a "traditional job" in order to pay the bills.

Until the voices started speaking to her.

No, she wasn't going crazy (although some may beg to differ). Bohannon realized that, up until this point, she had been all talk about caring about women's rights and social activism yet had very little track record to speak of. That's when she decided, in an idealistic spur of the moment, to purchase her one-way ticket to Uganda to start doing something about the unrelenting fire burning within her. One month later, she found herself in the hot and arid East African nation, armed with nothing but the phone number of an old acquaintance now living in Uganda and a thirst to discover something that would ease her insatiable desire for purpose and meaning.

She found it through disillusionment with the perceived ineptness of local non-profits and recalls "showing up and being very devastated" by the very colonial influence of the "giver vs. receiver" relationship between the Western world and Africa, a relationship dynamic that she felt had prohibited the continent from achieving actual success and independence. Having observed this good-intentioned yet simultaneously crippling approach to social impact, Bohannon vowed never to contribute to such means or methods, saying, "At that time I didn't have language or a vision for it but that has been something that has deeply influenced our work, everything from our legal structure to how we talk about our team and colleagues in Uganda."

Innovation

You may look at Sseko and wonder what is so innovative about it. After all, aren't there lots of companies that create products in countries of need in order to export them to wealthier developed countries to be sold? While this may be true now, it wasn't in 2009 when Sseko was started, and only a few fringe companies (like Toms Shoes) were operating in this type of business model.

Initially, Bohannon was advised by a friend/non-profit leader to begin Sseko by selling handmade paper beads, the infamously ubiquitous craft of choice for many Ugandans. Yet she couldn't get behind this worn-out (though historically productive) product line. "If I'm going to do this and I'm going to say we're going to solve a non-profit problem with a for-profit solution," said Bohannon, "I want to do that in a way that Nike looks at and goes, '*Hmmm*, interesting.'" She went on to state that "Ninety percent of the problems the non-profits are trying to solve would be solved if people had jobs with benefits. We're not going to get there if we keep making subpar products that people are buying out of a charitable mindset." Choosing instead to think outside the box eventually led to Sseko's current line of fashionable bags, sandals, and accessories. This pursuit of high-quality fashion products would propel Bohannon to push the boundary of the adjacent possible in the field of social impact business.

Advice
- **Just Do It**
    - Speaking of Nike, Bohannon says that "the percolating timer is up and you just need to do it!" There comes a point when, after allowing the creative juices to simmer and marinate, you just need to "level up," stop thinking, and start acting.
- **Make Mistakes**
    - It's okay to make mistakes. It wasn't until Bohannon started Sseko as a chicken farm (quite the transition from "birds" to "bags") that she learned she wasn't suited for agriculture. "You don't learn all those things by sitting behind a computer and googling and taking people out for informational interviews and taking them out for a cup of coffee."

Chapter 7

SHOW ME THE MONEY

*"The best way to predict the future is
to create it."
- Abraham Lincoln*

A Troublesome Paradox
Let's suppose I were to ask you to list the top three reasons why most people choose not to work in social impact. You would likely write something in regards to money. We live in a real world driven by sharp, prickly economic realities that too often seem to deflate the idealistic and altruistic explorations of so many well-intentioned men and women. We are all painfully aware of the harsh struggle for existence experienced by the one billion people in the world struggling to survive on less than one dollar a day; the harsh footprint mankind has left upon what is left of the world's ecosystem; and other seemingly inescapable terrible realities such as war, famine, and disease. While these realities continue to assail our desire for civility and equality, history has yet to deconstruct the supportive fabric that securely embeds these plagues within society. I would dare to say that good will and intention have never been lacking in great abundance within the hearts and minds of mankind as a whole. However, mankind's tired legs seem unable to escape the mire of a reality that seems pleased

to tantalize its inhabitants with fantasies of utopia while refusing to reveal its true identity.

What is the reason for this troublesome paradox? Why do man's best efforts over ages past fail to meet the mark of success and idealistic satisfaction? How has SID (and all social impact work) struggled so valiantly yet without substantial results to create this equalizing change in the world it so badly desires to bring about? The answer to this broad question is the even broader intrinsic reality of economics.

While social entrepreneurship is a vital component of contributing to the resolution of this ever-present issue of humanity, my strategy in circumnavigating this hot topic of economics is to present a mutually agreeable working understanding of economy's influence upon social impact fields in its most general sense in order to build upon that understanding a launch platform from which innovation may propel social entrepreneurship into greater heights through means of deeper understanding, creativity, and cultural relevance.

A Quick Economics Lesson
While certainly not revolutionary, the premise of this reality is simply this: for the consumption of a good or service, there must be an exchange of a perceived good or service of equal or greater value. In other words, "there ain't no such thing as a free lunch." If a good or service (such as design) is needed or desired, economics dictates that there must be a good or service of equal or greater value (such as a monetary fee) that must be exchanged for this good or service. This reality works seamlessly in the context of capable producers and consumers who have items that are mutually desired by the opposite agent in the economic transaction. The financially muscular tech company is fully capable of

providing its chosen architectural design firm with what is deemed as an equitable monetary compensation based upon the ability of that design firm to provide said company with a beneficial product. Most families with stable jobs and good health care can afford the occasional hospital visit. Countless venture capitalists are looking to fund the next young, talented entrepreneur with new, innovative technology that holds the promise of a lucrative return on investment.

In its broadest sense, this producer and consumer relationship is actually quite simple. Consumer (the tech company) desires a product (design for a building). Producer (the architecture firm) is able to give the consumer that product. If both the consumer and the producer are able to agree upon what value will be given for the cost received, there is mutual benefit and a transaction is created. Congratulations, I just saved you the cost of an ivy league MBA. Take that, Harvard.

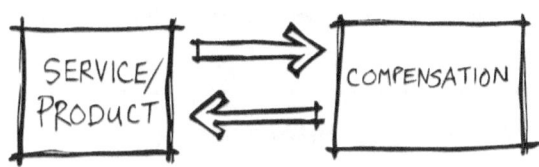

To pull this knowledge into our own context of SID, let's use refugees in need of infrastructure as our hypothetical consumer. The consumer desires a product, say clean running water. The producer, such as an engineer, is able to give the consumer that product. However, a wrench is now thrown into our economic machine. When it comes time to reach an agreed-upon exchange of equally valuable goods, the exchange is unequitable due to the fact that the refugee is incapable of

providing the producer with an equitable compensation.
    This raises an important concept of the idea of cost, one that we will focus heavily upon during this chapter. At first glance, this dilemma appears to be unsolvable based simply upon our overly simplistic concept of the exchange of goods and services from a producer to a consumer, yet SID embodies a powerful resistance to this concept, an outlier you might say. More often than not, SID is the manifestation of a consumer that is ill-equipped to provide an equally valuable compensation in exchange for the good or service he or she desires. This disparity can exist for any number of reasons including incompetence, volatile environments, and "acts of God" (a term used in architectural practice to mean uncontrollable natural forces in operation). Whatever the reason may be, said consumer is found to be incapable of providing the producer with a cost deemed of equal value (determined by society).
    This is where innovation kicks in.
    In light of the stalemate created within this transaction, one of social impact work's primary functions is to subsidize the perceived deficit within the transaction, typically through altruistic and charitable means. This subsidy can take many different forms such as government interaction, charitable donation, and pro bono. Whatever form it takes, it inherently involves absorption of what one might call the "debt" of the consumer by a separate (or similar) agent, resulting in a "zero loss" financial statement.
    Many freely criticize those equipped with talents and capacities of extraordinary measures (e.g., designers, doctors, lawyers) for not actively using those assets in pursuit of narrowing the gap between justice and its disparate counterpart. The reality of offering one's services or products at a lower than market rate value is

that the cost of that service or good is never negated; it is simply absorbed by another party. I am reminded of an analogy I once heard regarding the concept of debt:

When a man's newly constructed house is damaged by a neighboring driver, the driver begs the man to forgive him and simply act as if it never happened. What he doesn't understand is that while the homeowner may or may not choose to charge the driver for the damage he caused, it is impossible for that debt to simply be erased. If he chooses not to hold the man responsible for restoring his house to its original condition before the accident, he is simply choosing to either absorb the loss by suffering a damaged and perhaps unsafe house or he himself will be forced to pay for the repairs.

Economics in social entrepreneurship is the very foundation upon which we are to base our discussion of "designing your funding." In order to understand how social entrepreneurship is capable of advancing the threshold of the adjacent possible, it is critical to first understand that social impact work follows the same undeniable principles of economics that Goldman Sachs and IBM follow. IDEO founder Tim Brown states, "The willing and even enthusiastic acceptance of competing constraints is the foundation of design thinking."[1] If social impact fields are to experience the critical advancements in today's day and age which extraneous organizations and businesses are experiencing through innovation, they must come to a place of complete and utter acceptance of these unalterable economic forces.

Change in the Wind

Funding is often the reason why so many distance themselves from social impact work. When exchanging

---

1 Brown. *Change by Design*.

goods and services with resourceful consumers, one is most clearly able to provide for the needs of their person as well as their family (if applicable). It goes without saying that a worker is worth his wages. However, there seems to be an unshakeable aspect to social impact work that this desired, equitable state of security (most often gauged in financial terms) is unachievable or at least severely hampered. With this predicted inequitable quality of life in the minds of many with the thought of anticipated realities from working in SID, the field has remained grossly underpopulated and underdeveloped. The often non-existent prospect of economic prosperity in social impact fields has resulted in the continued rejection of this realm of work. Social impact work has inherited the same social status as the lovable college dropout who's always invited to parties but never financial strategy meetings.

    The great power found from innovating funding strategy within social entrepreneurship comes from the unique and exciting opportunities that have gone largely untapped in society. As previously mentioned, economics require an equal and opposite reaction, or "transaction" in our case, where a product is exchanged and the cost is given or absorbed by some party. For the remainder of this chapter, we will focus on opportunities to creatively approach economic needs for viable and sustainable social impact organizations. While SID and other social impact fields will likely never morph into the beautiful form of lucrative wealth-producing opportunities afforded in other avenues, I see the winds of opportunity beginning to blow within the sails of SID, the same winds that lie ready to propel all social entrepreneurs in their organizations.

Current SID industry innovators are operating in these three primary avenues:
- Legal Structure Options
- Alternative Customer Approaches
- Product Impact Reevaluation

Organizations have been making a powerful impact upon SID through these strategies, and they are signs of a changing industry, an industry that includes all social impact fields. The methods vary in their popularity and adaption into common practice, but they share the same connection to the zeitgeist of our information-dependent day and age.

Legal Structure Options

Before creating one's organization or company with which to use the power of SID, it is required by law that the entity choose a legal description by which to operate. There are several ways the government classifies an organization including various types of corporations (more on this later), partnerships, sole proprietorships, and non-profits. Each classification carries with it its own perks and liabilities.

Non-Profits (NPOs)
The most common classification within SID has typically been the non-profit, or the 501(c)(3).* A non-profit* (also known as a Non-Business Entity) is a legally recognized organization that "conducts business for the benefit of the general public without shareholders and without profit motive."[2] A common misconception regarding non-profits is that they are not allowed to or are incapable of generating income. While non-profits are seldom found on the top of the Fortune 500 list, these organizations are legally allowed to accumulate revenue so long as any revenue that exceeds the basic costs of the organization are poured back into the organization and not into the pockets of its members. Employees of non-profits are permitted to receive financial compensation for their work so long as it does not supersede typical market wages for that industry and specific position.

  The majority of organizations created with the overarching goal of creating SID such as MASS Design Group, Architecture for Humanity, 100 Fold Studio, and Impact Design Hub are categorized as a 501(c)(3). While employees of these organizations may not see the same level of lucrative compensation that employees of for-profit organizations might experience, their organization structure does come with certain benefits. In many countries, non-profits are allowed to file for tax-exempt status, granting them exemption from

---

2 TheFreeDictionary.com, s.v. "nonprofit," accessed 2018. https://legal-dictionary.thefreedictionary.com/nonprofit.

income, sales, property, and other possible taxes.

As I stated earlier, non-profit status does not inherently dictate its financial viability. At $40.3 billion as of the time of this writing, the Bill & Melinda Gates Foundation endowment is one of the largest in the US.[3] One of the major contributions to this and other non-profit organizations' financial capacity is due in part to charitable donations from outside sources because many (though not all) non-profits are allowed by the government to receive tax-exempt donations. After World War I, the US government implemented this charitable tax deduction. As of 2010, roughly 27 percent of Americans take advantage of this tax break.[4]

Corporations
The most common for-profit classification is called a corporation. In the legal sense, a corporation is a legal entity that is separate and distinct from its owners. This means that those financially invested in the ownership of the company—its shareholders—are allowed to partake in the profits produced by that company through its dividends while not being financially responsible for the debts of the organization. Corporations operate under the directive that the company's sole objective is to pursue a purpose commonly agreed upon by its shareholders. While this purpose may vary depending on the type of corporation (we will discuss this shortly), they are typically set up with the primary objective of providing its shareholders with a financial return.

Corporations are legally bound to pursue the vested interests of their shareholders, which is, in essence, the secret sauce to capitalism's success. The freedom to pursue greater profits not allowed to non-profits

---

3 "Bill and Melinda Gates Foundation"
4 "Charitable Contributions"

is typically accredited with the high degree of motivation and drive with which corporations operate in running their organization.

While corporations are not typically paired with the concept of philanthropy in the minds of most, there are various ways that corporations can be a part of SID, though many sources state the amount of corporation philanthropy has been in steady decline over the past couple of decades. In 2002, the *Harvard Business Review* claimed that corporate charitable contributions declined by 14.5 percent from the last year and 50 percent since 1987.[5] Recent times seem to confirm that trend, partially due to the common obligation of a corporation to prioritize the interests of its shareholders, which often leave little room for charitable pursuits. In order to solve the organizational hardship of creating social impact, many corporations choose to form a separate 501(c)(3) organization with the sole purpose of enacting the social good that corporation wishes to promote despite its corporate hurdles.

I experienced this process firsthand in a firm I once worked for. With more than 400 employees across the country, the organization found it difficult to create lasting impact even though we considered ourselves a very socially minded design firm. The other difficulty we faced was cohesion. Since SID was not one of the company's critical priorities, it remained a scattered and relatively unorganized effort to utilize our design capabilities for promoting social good. During the process of pursuing a more organized manner of creating social good, we found it to be a common practice amongst similar firms to create a non-profit or "foundation" which could then be funded by the corporation but operate with more autonomy and greater clarity.

5 Porter. "The Competitive Advantage."

However, while it is clearly possible to participate in SID from within the structure of a corporation, many have found it severely limiting in terms of capacity. You might remember from the previous chapter that a common goal for corporate philanthropy is 1 percent, which is nothing to be discounted. Despite the collective potential found within the realm of corporate philanthropy, there remained a deep sense of dissatisfaction for many who found themselves working for an organization with expectant shareholders while simultaneously working to achieve some form of social good.

That's why the Benefit Corporation* was born.

B-Corp to the Rescue

In 2010, the US officially recognized its first Benefit Corporation (B Corps) as a legitimate legal organization. B Corps are similar to a traditional C Corporation in its taxation but differ in their purpose, transparency, and accountability. They exist with the purpose to not only compete to be the best in the world but also the best for the world. Today, there are more than 2,000 certified B Corps spanning across the globe in fifty countries and more than 130 industries.[6] Some of those organizations you may recognize include Patagonia (outdoor apparel), Kickstarter (crowdfunding), and Ben and Jerry's (spoonfuls of heavenly bliss). This new business structure is a revolutionary innovation in how social impact is done beginning from the ground up, the very essence upon which this book is about.

The B Corps legal structure is revolutionary in that it allows a corporation to pick any social cause, whether that be providing nutritious meals to lower-income families or protecting the environment from

---

6 B Lab. "Year in Review."

degradation, and essentially treat that cause as a legitimate opinion-holding shareholder in the organization. No longer are the members of these for-profit organizations bound solely to enact decisions that will increase shareholder's dividends, instead allowing for the company to redefine what success looks like. It's almost as if the social cause championed by the B Corp becomes a major shareholder whose opinion carries great weight in decision making.

B Corps share a striking resemblance to SID in the sense that they both employ sustainable means toward achieving positive ends. B Corps can either begin with their cause being the primary driving factor or they can be a transitional move from a traditional corporation to a different structure type that provides greater protection for their efforts to promote their cause. In other words, it combines the cause (social impact) and the means through which to promote that cause (in our case, design).

SID is not bound to any one of these organization types specifically, but the story behind the formation of the B Corp stands as a testimony to the necessity and exciting possibility with innovation. The B Corp structure represents a design approach to a very solvable problem that merely required someone with the courage and initiative to step back and truly analyze all available tools and possibilities in solving a problem. If social impact design-

> *B Corps share a striking resemblance to SID in the sense that they both employ sustainable means toward achieving positive ends.*

ers choose to look at the world through the same lens that brought this solution into focus, "design-before-design" solutions will continue to become more and more apparent to all social entrepreneurs as more tools, strategies, and opportunities become available.

Alternative Customer Approaches

"I just look at how conventional banks do it. Once I learned how they do it, I just did the opposite. And it worked!"[7]

Typical, everyday transactions can represent some of the paradigms we hold regarding equitable compensation for goods and services.

As an architect, I work in a service industry that provides clients primarily with non-material goods, our design services. In exchange for this service, our client then reimburses us for our service with an agreed-upon amount of financial compensation within agreed-upon periods of time. Upon receiving this compensation, my employer then disperses a portion of this compensation to its employees, one of which is yours truly. Because I contributed my services to my company's client, it was mutually agreed upon that I should receive an equitable level of compensation for that work that matches common market earnings of architects with my level of training and experience.

When purchasing food and drinks at a restaurant, I am on the other end of the worker/client relationship by providing an agreed-upon amount of financial compensation for the culinary goods and services. Through

---

7 TEDx. "A History of Microfinance."

means of financial transaction, I the customer am able to enjoy the fruits of the restaurant's labor (pun intended) while the restaurant is able to reasonably expect a monetary compensation for their work, contributing to their revenue stream which then supports their business needs.

Architecture is an industry that provides a typically high-quality service and, therefore, an equally high monetary compensation. It's worth pointing out that that world history has often left SID out of its story telling, choosing instead to share tales of the relationship between design and the world's more affluent citizens. I'm sure you can think of other fields besides architecture where the same is true. In essence, it has become common knowledge that customers worthy of high-quality service or goods must equally possess high levels of power, money, and/or influence. Without these assets, common understanding of commerce would essentially justify the denial of these goods and/or services to the customers in the shallower end of the financial resource pool.

The cry of this book is not one of political or moral observations but that of self-empowerment, a mantra that explains how innovation provides social entrepreneurs the power with which to pull upon incredible amounts of untapped potential. We only lack the congruency to piece together the power of our combined design prowess and tenacity. Author Austin Kleon labeled the person who pulled from this creative power of the collective a "scenius," or one who heightens the power of his creative "genius" through the collective influences of those around him, his social "scene."[8]

The ordinary maintains; the innovative propels. The ordinary approach to customers and financial op-

---

8 Kleon. *Steal like an Artist.*

SCENE + GENIUS
=
SCENIUS

portunity, particularly in the realm of design, has left us with the common mindset that while philanthropic idealism is cute, it's literally a poor way to live. The typical producer/consumer relationship has largely led to this mindset due in large part to unquestioned assumptions we have made regarding this system. There are two common assumptions about the structure of the producer/consumer relationship that are now being challenged in today's innovative age: (1) altruistic efforts are incapable of contributing to revenue generation, and (2) financially poor consumers are incapable of providing producers sufficient compensation to generate profit.

The ordinary maintains; the innovative propels.

Business of Opposites

The world was not always as interconnected and globally minded as it is today. By nature of available technology, cultures, and economies, previous societies were inherently more exclusive and isolated. Trade happened within one's village with individual customers as communication and transportation were far too limiting to think outside of one's immediate sphere of influence. As technology has evolved, so has society's ability to influence and be influenced by those far outside their physical proximity while being inside their digital proximity. We are now a global economy, and in many areas, this mindset of viewing possible markets with a wider lens has become more fully embraced. Within the realm of social impact, this mindset holds great power to change how the client of social impact services can essentially be reevaluated.

At the beginning of this section, I gave a quote by Muhammad Yunus, an economist and social entrepreneur who came up with the crazy idea of doing the opposite of the most financially successful money institutions. You might have heard of this influential man from Bangladesh commonly known as the father of microfinance. Yunus was awarded the 2006 Nobel peace prize for the creation of the revolutionary bank Grameen Bank, commonly known as "the bank for the poor."[9]

Yunus's story really began upon returning to his native Bangladesh after receiving his doctorate in economics from the US. He found himself privileged with a comfortable university professor position but was shocked at the abject poverty of his nation just outside of his comfortable sphere of influence. Yunus's subsequent investigation led him to discover that laziness was not the source of this poverty, as he saw countless hard working men and women all around him still confined to a life void of economic return. Instead, after interviewing forty-two people from one village, Yunus discovered to his horror that what kept many of these hard-working entrepreneurs from achieving financial

9 TEDx. "A History of Microfinance."

freedom was the mere $27 that many of them needed to finance their businesses. In fact, one woman who made hand-crafted stools was unable to escape poverty for lack of five cents required for her to purchase her supplies each day. It didn't take long to recognize the antagonist of the story. Local loan sharks were the only forms of available capital, and they preyed upon their impoverished customers due to the lack of corporate oversight over these companies, allowing them to charge up to 1,000 percent interest on any one loan. With such outrageous interest rates, villagers were essentially forced into business slavery, never being able to free themselves from their financial bondage.

Yunus applied the tool of innovation to design a solution to alleviate his people's suffering. "In order to solve problems I started creating businesses. It almost became instinctive in me. Whenever I saw a problem, I went right ahead and designed a business to solve the problem."[10] In pursuit of time-proven methods of generating revenue, the local banks had chosen to work exclusively with those wealthy clients who appeared to be the only source of viable income. While no one would likely disagree that this was perhaps the best route for maximizing financial gain, Yunus was motivated more by his desire to solve a social and humanitarian need than to simply focus on maxing out his net worth.

He created a banking system that would not only generate sustainable profit but would also contribute to the solution for the problem he saw, and he did it by re-evaluating his approach to customers. "I just look at the conventional banks, how they do it. Once I learned how they do it, I just did the opposite. And it worked! They go to the rich people, so I go to the poor people. They go to men, so I go to women. They go to the city cen-

---

10 TEDx. "A History of Microfinance."

ter businesses, I wanted to go to the remote village."[11] Many looked at him as if he was committing financial suicide with this approach to banking. Nobody in their right mind could possibly expect to create a financially viable institution that worked exclusively with the most impoverished and underserved members of the population, yet Grameen Bank stands to this day as a sharp counter rebuttal to this traditional mindset. As of December 2018, Grameen Bank proudly boasts substantial numbers that prove its viability: 9 million members (8.8 million of which are women); USD $26.6 billion of loans since its inception, 91.5 percent of which have been fully recovered; more than 70,000 beggars are currently being served with the provision of business microloans, 22,000 of which were able to stop begging between 2007 and 2012; and 734,991 houses built through housing loans.[12]

Yunus employed social creativity to discover that there were extremely viable and business-savvy alternatives to the traditional approach to customers. Beginning with an aspiration to use business to solve problems for his own people and empowered by the presence of technology and intellectual creativity and fortitude, he innovated a whole new methodology to approaching business for social impact, stating, "Human creativity and capacity is limitless…This is the age where we all have this capacity of technology. The question is do we have the *methodology* of using this capacity to address these problems"[13] [emphasis added].

Social impact design strategist Wendy Woods sees those very same social impact opportunities within business, saying that "one of the best ways for business-

---

11 TEDx. "A History of Microfinance."
12 "Monthly Report: 2019-01 Issue 469 in USD"
13 TEDx. "A History of Microfinance."

es to help ensure their own growth, their own longevity, is to meet some of the hardest challenges in our society and to do so profitably."[14] Just as Yunus found a way to create profit from meeting one of the hardest challenges in his home of Bangladesh with Grameen Bank, Woods points to South Africa's Standard Bank as an example of business driven by social impact. In South Africa, government regulations require that all banks donate .2 percent of their profits to black-owned small and medium enterprises. While most banks do this through the quick and easy charitable donation, Woods highlights how Standard Bank has stood apart in their innovative approach to the prompt. Standard Bank chose to instead use their funds to create a trust that could then provide loans to black South African entrepreneurs. "More entrepreneurs supported, more people and communities being lifted out of poverty,"[15] Woods says. This business model has allowed the bank to support more businesses and with greater investment on their part since the bank intentionally tied their profitability with that of the entrepreneurs they serve.

Like Grameen and Standard Bank, many organizations and entrepreneurs have the same desire to help people in need. However, the approach taken by

> *"One of the best ways for businesses to help ensure their own growth...is to meet some of the hardest challenges in our society and to do so profitably."*
> - Wendy Woods

---

14 Woods. "The Business Benefits."
15 Woods

these two financial institutions stand as a testimony to the power of human innovation in solving actual world problems through sustainable, scalable strategies. While certainly commendable, traditional businesses would probably have approached these needs from a different angle. The tendency is to compartmentalize revenue generating streams from altruistic efforts, treating the altruism as a leech requiring unmerited sustenance while giving nothing in return. Through the efforts of bold social impact institutions like these banks, new opportunities for more socially impactful enterprises are now being opened up.

Double Bottom Line

John Levy is a financer, entrepreneur, and the current chairman of the board at a company called BioLite, but his journey into the issue of sustainable social impact started long ago on the streets of New York. While volunteering at a homeless shelter, Levy found himself dissatisfied with the results of the shelter. As always, the shelter had the best of intentions to serve the city's underserved, but Levy saw an inherent flaw in the system when he saw the homeless viewing the shelter as the ultimate solution to their problem and not merely a transitional tool to help them get their feet back underneath them. This realization of the organization's inability to propel its constituents to greater self-sustaining heights set him on a journey of questioning how one could speak life to society's underprivileged while not diminishing them in the same breath.[16]

After leaving two venture capital funds, he started in New York to pursue ways of using his skills and abilities to fight global climate change. Levy met Jonathan Cedar and Alec Drummond, two young men who would

16 TEDx. "What the World Doesn't Need."

eventually come to form BioLite, a company focused on creating innovative products that "transform the way we Cook, Charge and Light our lives off the grid."[17] Having met in 2008 at a combustion conference, Jonathan and Alec were excited about their innovative new cook stove that not only reduced toxic carbon emissions by 90 percent but also generated electricity by means of heat generation. Their design even won an award for the cleanest stove at the conference. With this in mind, Levy realized that what they had created was not merely a more efficient stove but rather an economically viable product for bringing power to the 2.3 billion people with little to no access to electricity (many people in developing countries pay 20–30 percent of their income on utilities, in contrast to 4 percent that Americans pay). Realizing that, in their search for a fuel-efficient stove, they had stumbled upon an off-grid energy company presented them with new exciting possibilities. "If we got it right, we could harness a tremendous social mission on a very interesting business model."[18]

So the BioLite team embarked upon a daring new business model that, much like the B Corp philosophy, would combine a socially guided mission with a financially sustainable and profitable business strategy to create an enterprise that, unlike previous socially minded entities Levy had worked with, could be scalable at the global level.

For example, the idea of providing developing countries with products that provided them with electricity and dramatically reduced the more than four million annual deaths from cooking smoke-related diseases sounds an awful lot like the work of NGOs (Non-Government Organizations).* Many aid organiza-

---

17 "Our Story – The BioLite History."
18 TEDx. "What the World Doesn't Need."

tions are known for heroic efforts to insert themselves into underdeveloped nations where such technology is needed more than anywhere else, often for free. However, Levy had identified several problems with this methodology: First, providing valuable products without any form of compensation often led to undervaluing that product, essentially establishing the inherent value of the product at $0. Second, it also created a shortage of supply since the products could only be distributed in between fundraising, which could take substantial amounts of time. Finally, a great opportunity to provide local employment by creating businesses to distribute the product was missed.

Hence, BioLite found that viewing those in need of their product as customers in lieu of beggars created the basis upon which BioLite would create its financial structure. "If we could build a company based on a true high value product, we made it affordable and available, we had the potential to serve an incredible social mission,"[19] says Levy, referring to this as a "double bottom line" business model. What this means is that, much like a business can measure its financial bottom line through measuring and calculating data streams such as revenue, expenses, net profit, and return on investment, it is equally feasible to measure a business' social

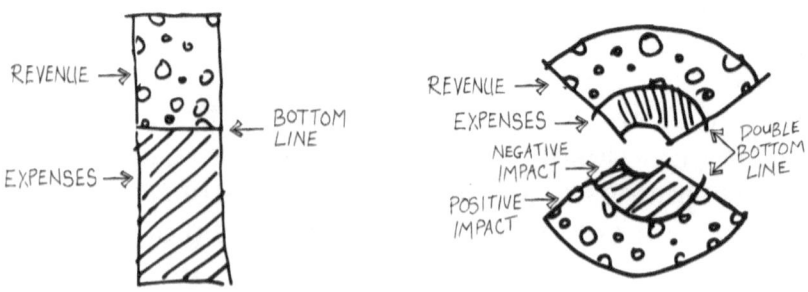

19 TEDx. "What the World Doesn't Need."

bottom line through metrics such as carbon output, mortality rate, energy costs, and household savings.

Product Impact Reevaluation
Wrong Hole
A direct client relationship is a transaction of monetary goods for a product, and nearly every financial transaction we can think of could be considered direct. Regardless of whether the client is an individual or a multination corporation, it is relatively clear to identify the product or service being purchased and the two entities between whom it is being transferred in this type of direct client transaction.

It is because of this standard of direct client transaction we have come to understand as normal in economics that social impact work has often appeared to be the "grown-up" kid whom no one takes seriously, the renegade rule breaker of societal and economic norms. Thus, the direct client relationship formula we know and grasp simply doesn't fit the sometimes annoying constraints SID has embraced as inevitable.

Imagine a child playing with one of those hollow balls filled with voids of varying shapes and sizes. The child knows perfectly well that the square block in his or her hand perfectly fits the void matching those exact dimensions on the block, allowing him or her to seamlessly drop the object into the center of the toy, much to his or her great delight. However, upon reaching the hexagon-shaped void adjacent, he or she tries to no avail to fit that same square piece in the new void, eventually resorting to dropping an unsubstantial marble inside the hole, thinking that that measly object, though vastly out of scale to its hexagonal port of entry, is simply the best he can fit inside the hole. Yet unbeknownst to the child, a perfectly sized hexagonal block lies just out of sight and out of mind.

In much the same way, an exasperated world has treated social impact fields as that hexagon-shaped hole, an inconvenient entanglement preventing us from depositing our nice and neat square-shaped void inside of it. As if indignant of this unacceptable problem, we have resorted to dropping marbles into the hole, satisfied that that was the best that could be done. However, some social innovators such as John Hudson have found a new hexagon, and for Hudson, it came in the form of embracing the atypical "indirect" client relationship.

In the previous chapter, we discussed Hudson and how he designed the purpose of 100 Fold Studio, but that wasn't the only innovative approach 100 Fold Studio took to designing its organization. Unlike Grameen Bank and BioLite, 100 Fold Studio is a non-profit organization, meaning that its funding sources are somewhat more limited than that of a typical business. Currently, 100 Fold Studio receives its funding from various sources including design fees (a minimal amount as the firm works at significantly reduced fees), grants, and donations. At first glance, this may not seem all that innovative, but within the framework, Hudson has done something to alter how it approaches donations as a source of funding.

If you've ever fundraised for an organization, you know it can be exhausting. There is often a certain feeling of begging when approaching individuals or organizations and asking them for their money. This is often the approach many non-profits feel forced to take when supplying their needs to fulfill their vision, and it has left many, including both donors and recipients, feeling disenchanted and bitter toward the whole idea, a feeling not too far off from that of the child sitting in defeat after his hexagon-block-in-a-square-hole catastrophe.

Hudson and others like him have begun to re-evaluate not only the purpose for which they exist and the service they subsequently provide but also the type of client relationship with which to do business and achieve their desired social impact. While the direct client relationship, in which the good or service transfers hands directly from the producer to the consumer, is the standard, 100 Fold Studio has embraced what I call an "indirect" client relationship. What this means is that instead of thinking of the users or organizations in need of design services as the sole client, 100 Fold Studio has started to look outward. While not ignoring the direct relationship with the organization or building occupants that would eventually inhabit the finished architectural product (those relationships will always be integral), they have expanded the pool of their clientele to include people with a desire to be a part of creating social impact while also having financial capacity. In other words, they stepped away from the tree trunk in order to **reevaluate** who was actually being **impacted** by the "**product**" they offered.

There are countless men and women outside of these organizations' direct circle of interaction who inherently desire to be a part of the mission that 100 Fold Studio promotes. However, due to an extensive amount of possible reasons, they themselves are incapable of directly providing that social impact that they wish to see. However, in economic terms, they still provide a "demand" for that service and are simply in search of a "supply."

That's where the indirect client relationship is born.

100 Fold Studio searches out those clients "demanding" the enacting of SID that they wish to see but are themselves unable to produce and essentially step in to provide that desired service. As a hypothetical example, Joe Smith is a banker who lives in Cincinnati and hears about what 100 Fold Studio is doing all over the world by providing free and discounted architectural services to organizations in need. Joe has always loved architecture and helping people, but he always felt his skill set was more toward numbers instead of design. Joe is thrilled when he finds out someone exists out there that can make the impact on the world that he always wished he could be a part of—and now he can! By becoming an indirect client of 100 Fold Studio, Joe can continue doing what he is most gifted at (banking) while receiving the satisfaction

> *Economies that thrive are defined by their adherence to organic financial principles.*

of playing an important role in promoting SID through the work of 100 Fold Studio.

Resistance Is Futile
What 100 Fold Studio and organizations like it do is far from a bell-ringing guy dressed as Santa Claus in front of the shopping mall asking for spare change in a red bucket (mad respect to all who do that in the frigid Montana winters). In fact, you might say it is the difference between placing a marble and a hexagonal block through the hexagon-shaped hole. They can both fit, but one of them clearly fits better than the other. Economies that thrive are defined by their adherence to organic financial principles (i.e, supply and demand). Economies that flounder are those that resist these laws by trying to manipulate the principles into shapes they were never meant to be.

Integrating the indirect client principle into 100 Fold's operating strategy switches out the marble for the hexagon block. This innovative approach to non-profit funding promotes vitality because it more closely aligns to the naturally occurring financial principles within for-profit businesses. As one of 100 Fold's partners in achieving their mission, I can personally attest to the very real difference between being asked for money versus being offering a service that integrates me into the impact they are creating.

A clear example of this was this past summer when I was invited to participate in a 100 Fold Studio partners trip to Battambang, Cambodia, the location of their currently ongoing campus construction project for YWAM. While our group of more than thirty organizational partners spent a week on the base, we were able to experience firsthand the impact this project is making upon the Cambodian people. Seeing everything from the cafeteria, capable of handling hundreds of local and international students, to walking through the beautiful and energy-efficient community training center where untold numbers of local Cambodians will come to learn valuable life and career skills tangibly reminded me that my investment in 100 Fold is more than just a charitable contribution that I write off on my taxes at the end of the year. Instead, it represents the incredible fact that I am able to enter into a "business" transaction that helps bring about incredible social impact, a service I greatly value and find unequivocally worthy of my financial participation.

No Promises, Starbucks
SID's embrace of indirect client relationships can stand as one of several observable and repeatable tools for obtaining the same types of growth and success that innovative organizations in other fields have already experienced. "100 Fold is not trying to be charitable architecture,"[20] says John Hudson, explaining that they might have started in that direction but have since then discovered the opportunity to create participation in their firm's ultimate objective, one which is shared by many current and future "clients" all over the world. I remember sitting down with Hudson one time and hearing him explain to me that organizations like 100 Fold were just as much of a business as companies like Starbucks. While it may seem guaranteed, Starbucks, like any other business, is never given 100 percent assurance that a customer will walk through those doors when they open early each morning. All they can do is continue to offer their client base a product that they perceive as desirable and operate in good faith that customers will con-

---

20 John Hudson (Founder, 100 Fold Studio), interviewed by Jacob DeNeui in Battambang, Cambodia, July 14, 2017.

tinue to walk through that door and ask to purchase a cup of coffee-flavored milk and sugar.

Bridges and Boundaries

Companies and organizations like Grameen Bank, BioLite, and 100 Fold Studio serve as beacons in the quest toward greater competency and capacity within social entrepreneurship through the creative and innovative reevaluation of customer and market approach. No longer are companies limited to markets composed of exclusively "wealthy" clients. Instead, new SID ventures are pushing the boundaries of the adjacent possible. Think of it like a bridge that is being built over a large body of water, its length growing every day as new concrete supports and sections are added to its length. While very few find themselves at the "cutting edge" of that new bridge, the few that do are exposed to entirely new points of views and scenes never before viewed by humans. In the same way, organizations such as these serve as explorers of the ever-expanding frontier, the beholders of these new and exciting moments in time that will someday serve as the platform upon which

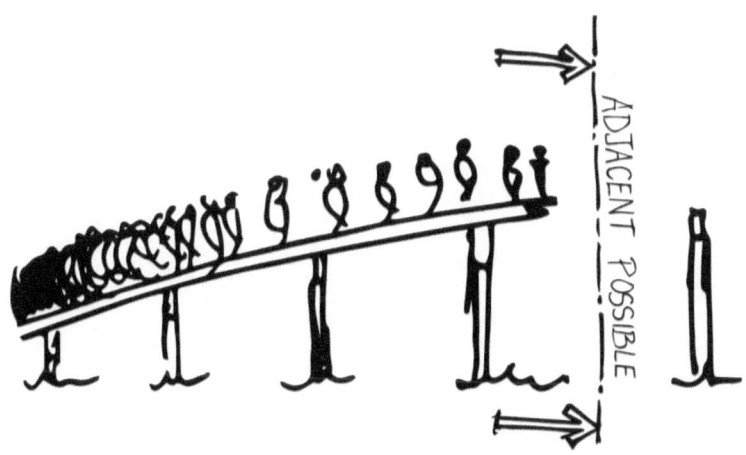

other new and innovative ideas and practices can be propelled. Reframing our understanding of untapped and underdeveloped markets is simply one bridge of innovation upon which SID is currently expanding its realm of possible influence, but it is one in which I still see significant amounts of yet unexplored views.

Chapter 7 in a page...

- Since "debt" can never be erased, only absorbed, design that is given without equitable reimbursement (typically SID) often leaves someone else paying the tab
- Successful social impact financial models follow natural economic principles
- 501(c)(3), or non-profits, are the most common legal structure in social impact organizations
- Corporations do not inherently exclude the possibility of social impact but they tend to create significant restrictions
- **Benefit Corporations**, or B Corps, are an innovative new legal structure that protect the organization's freedom to promote a chosen social cause
- Grameen Bank and BioLite pursued impoverished customers in order to tap unreached markets while creating sustainable social impact
- 100 Fold Studio took "charity" and turned it into "business" by embracing an atypical **indirect** client relationship

Food for Thought...

1. Paint a picture of what your organization could look like as a corporation, non-profit, or B Corps (or explore others if you want). Do you see any benefits to one over the other?
2. Describe your organization's avatar. Who do you serve and why? Now think of an entirely new client that you might never have considered before. What would your organization look like if you served them? Or both?
3. Is your proposed business model based on direct or indirect client relationships? Flip it around and see what it would look like then.

Chapter 8

HARDER, BETTER, FASTER, STRONGER

"Discovery consists of seeing what everybody has seen and thinking what nobody has thought."
- Albert Szent-Györgyi

Click, Click, CLACK!
Imagine for a moment you and several of your colleagues are taken hostage by foreign armed forces inside a bank. You are all locked inside the entry room into the primary vault, including a mysterious government agent who seems to have a knack for getting out of trouble. However, when the militia leader departs from your locked room with a little gift, a timed explosive, you know the end is near. The door is locked, and the only chance of safety lies behind a sixteen-inch-thick locked vault door. Before even a tear can be shed, the government agent leaps into action, shattering the despairing mood.

    At first, your heart can't help but hope as his quick response must indicate that some form of rescue plan is moments away from being pulled from his resourceful mind. He begins to frantically tear the room apart, beginning with the small intercom system mounted on the wall next to the door, then moving on to the telephone on the adjacent table. Your despair returns, realizing the terror of the situation must have made him lose his marbles. *What in God's name does this poor man think he's doing?* you think to yourself as he continues his desperate antics, pulling the poor, mutilated bodies of formerly functioning electronics toward the vault door and continuing his ravenously destructive spree of yanking and tearing, twisting and ripping. Despite the futility of his wanton actions, you can't help but stare at him in anticipation, seconds passing faster and faster, his fingers moving in quick but deliberate movements.

As you see him transform the jumble of exposed wiry guts into what appears to be a grossly mutated yet possibly useful contraption, a glimmer of hope suddenly returns. He springs to his feet, broken phone in hand, rushes toward the vault door, plants the phone against the door, and begins to spin the lock's dial—the number ":28" eerily plastered across the bomb's digital screen. *Click, click, click, CLACK!* You jump when the man shouts for joy upon hearing the mutilated intercom speaker shout out a loud confirmation of successfully finding the vault's first of three numerical combination digits. With the seconds counting down, all eyes are now glued on the vault door, the only chance for survival. *Click, click, click, click, click, CLACK!* The room releases an anxious yet joyful shout at the signal that one digit now remains. Three seconds and six clicks later and *EUREKA!* The lock is open. Now, with but five—now four—seconds left, he viciously spins the vault handle and pulls open the door with all his might, its movement tauntingly slow. Your coworker hands him the bomb and without hesitation, he throws it into the vault. He quickly recounts his efforts, sealing the vault and ensuring their safety. No sooner does the metal door return to its sealed state that the bomb detonates, rocking the whole room yet leaving you, your coworkers, and MacGyver (the government agent) safe and sound.

Bombs and Paper Clips

If you've ever watched the show MacGyver, this scene is a typical demonstration of the show's protagonist Angus MacGyver's uncanny ability to save the day by transforming everyday, seemingly useless tools into resourceful and timely apparatuses. The show's character became so iconic for this ability, in fact, that the word *MacGyver* is now included in the Oxford Dictionary as a verb meaning "to make or repair (an object) in an improvised or inventive way, making use of whatever items are at hand." While the original MacGyver show aired from 1987–1992, our fascination with a hero known for his fascinating ability to contrive amazing inventions and contraptions out of items that seemed completely irrelevant and unrelated spurred Hollywood to bring back the famous MacGyver story with an entirely new cast twenty-four years later. After all, who doesn't want to watch a guy diffuse a bomb with a paper clip?

In a way, Sid (from our own adventure story) and MacGyver share a similar hardwiring that sets them apart from so many others around them. While the majority of people in MacGyver's situation would simply overlook the paper clip in their search for a clear-cut solution like a key, a gun, or a chainsaw (just throwing stuff out there), characters like Sid and MacGyver have the exciting ability to spot patterns and connections. It's not an ability you can just teach from a book but rather a skill set that must be developed and strengthened through practice.

Creativity is simply the ability to identify patterns. Whether it be music, painting, architecture, or fashion, what we identify as creativity is simply a person's ability to materialize their unique understanding of some form of patterns that exist all around us. Creative people are like radios in that they perceive patterns like radio waves, a steady and constant flow of information that is always around us, but only once it is captured and audibly reproduced by the radio can it be perceived and enjoyed by the human mind.

Creativity is enjoyed primarily outside of SID and other social impact fields due to the fact that social entrepreneurs often dismiss many creative solutions by assuming that tools employed by non-SID entities are invalid or impractical for social impact work. This is a misconception bred by belief that highly innovative and cutting-edge tools and technology are monetarily out of reach for those focusing on utilizing their skill sets primarily to achieve social good.

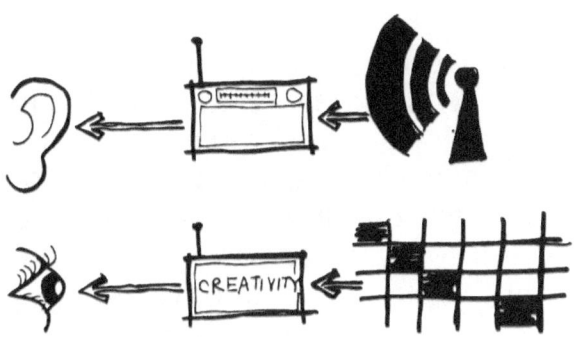

When in Rome
What if innovation was a primary tool that empowered social entrepreneurs to meet the needs of those in the world who carry the deepest needs? Oddly enough, it used to be.

Students, it's time for a quick history lesson on how advances in design and technology were literally the building blocks of an architecture that promoted social equality. Please open your textbooks to chapter 200 (200 BC, that is) as we jump back in time to visit the architectural masterpiece known as ancient Rome.

While history shows that civilizations such as the Chinese had discovered the incredible structural benefits of calcifying lime-based mortars (cement), Rome is credited with adding aggregate to the cement mix to create what is now known as concrete, or "opus caementicium" as it was known to the Romans. This combination of cement and aggregate allowed for the vast size and large-scale implementation of developments such as the Colosseum as well as smaller building projects such as the residential "insula."[1]

> *Creativity is simply the ability to identify patterns.*

The significance of this architectural and engineering breakthrough lies in the social and philosophical effect it had when executed within Rome's urban fabric. The insula was a multi-story housing unit for common Roman citizens, standing up to four stories tall. While incredible in its application of advanced engineering and construction technology, what is most fascinating for the purpose of our discussion is the social implications created by this building typology. While multi-story housing units like the insula were understandably not built to the same health and welfare standards that we enjoy today, its inception stands as a historical testament to the power of innovation in its intimate relationship with SID. This innovation in construction technology was not reserved for just the wealthy and elite but for all Roman citizens, illustrating two ingrained beliefs in Roman society: people matter, regardless of economic status, and the distribution of quality design tangibly demonstrates this value. Granted, there were certainly still aspects of ancient Roman

---

1 Becker. "Roman Domestic Architecture (insula)."

society that created less than a positive social impact. (I doubt Caesar got much fan mail from his enslaved gladiators.) Despite Rome's undeniably militant nature, woven into its very urban fabric was the belief that it is humanity, not status, that merits good design. Interestingly enough, it was the resources that Roman architects, builders, and city planners utilized that contributed to the manifestation of a society that intrinsically valued public architecture.

> *People matter, regardless of economic status, and the distribution of quality design tangibly demonstrates this value.*

Fingerprints of a Dream
Now we return to the 21st century.

Gone is the belief that forward thinking and the advancement of human flourishing could be blind to social status. In the words of one designer, "We grow so accustomed to the notion that doctors' offices and affordable housing developments can only be drab and unoriginal environments that we don't even dare to dream that they could reflect and bolster the spirits of those who frequent them."[2] It seems our society as a whole has ceased to believe that such passion and zeal, such visionary optimism and idealism, could ever be used for SID's humble yet noble purposes.

We don't even dare to dream.

What if more social entrepreneurs dared to dream? What if designers, teachers, lawyers, and oth-

2 Cary. The Power of Pro Bono.

er workers committed to using their skill sets to create social impact across the spectrum stopped assuming that certain tools were off limits simply because initial assumptions stated that such tools weren't economically feasible for their work?

What if more social entrepreneurs **designed** their **resources**?

I say "more" because, thankfully, there are already noteworthy efforts being made specifically within SID to bring cutting-edge technology and innovation into SID's tool belt, too noteworthy not to share with other social entrepreneurs. One such enterprise is a small, innovative tech company out of the UK that is revolutionizing the realm of biometric technology, all based on the belief that people matter.

> *What if more social entrepreneurs dared to dream?*

When the founders of Simprints recognized the huge problem that existed for 1.5 billion people living without any formal identification—mostly those living in slums across developing parts of the world—they decided to harness their skill sets to design a mobile fingerprint scanning solution with the intent of being utilized by medical workers in developing countries in order to access the digital health records of patients. Simprints was certainly not the first company to attempt to solve this great need for identification, yet they found their innovative solution to be the key to solving the gross inefficiencies and faults in existing technology. The result was a solution that was four times cheaper and 228 percent more accurate than other available solutions. Where other solutions had failed because of inability to respond to existing constraints due to limited available local systems and technology, Simprints succeeded by creating a solution that could either seamlessly integrate into an existing system or stand alone. In essence, their design supported rather than duplicated existing government efforts.

Simprints has found itself on the cusp of the adjacent possible, and the world has noticed. Its impressive advancements in biometric technology have caught the eyes of and received accolades from numerous entities including *Business Weekly*'s 2015 Startup of the Year, UNICEF & TechCrunch Award for Best Tech, and *Forbes* 30 Under 30 Social Entrepreneurs. These recognitions are not unmerited.

Who would have thought that a young tech company focused on giving the gift of identity to the impoverished and destitute of the world would be on the forefront of biometric technology? Perhaps this is in part due to Simprints's founder and CEO Toby Norman's decision to design his funding to create a strong, sustainable platform that would bolster the likelihood of successfully using design to bring about social impact. Norman states that Simprints "chose to be a limited shares company with an asset lock as it seemed an innovative way to secure funds now with the option of attracting investors in the future," focusing on business grants to "get us off the ground while committing to our social-impact focus..."[3] Simprints serves as a prime example of how an organization intent on changing the world through design can and has done so by designing both their funding and their resources.

Lo-Fab
In 2010, Haiti was rocked by devastating earthquakes. While $10 billion in aid was given to the country, very

---

3 Manhart and Millar. "Building a Social Enterprise."

little went directly into the hands of locals. This unfortunately inhibited the nation from building sustainable businesses and practices that would help them combat such disasters without outside aid, contributing to the continuance of disease and poverty even five years later. MASS Design Group[4] chose to intervene but in a different way. Often in social impact work, it is assumed that the recipients of the work are to be treated as helpless charity cases, incapable of aiding in their own rescue and recovery. To debunk this antiquated colonial mindset toward social impact is outside the range of this book, yet its presence is still a force to be reckoned with in social entrepreneurs' struggle to innovate.

So what exactly did MASS do that so strongly opposed the standard practice of design intervention in humanitarian aid?

One word: **"lo-fab"**

MASS has used this term to describe their practice of "LOcal FABrication,"[5] and it has become integral to the transformative impact their design work has had upon local communities. MASS has holistically adopted lo-fab into their design process by considering and implementing local construction typologies from the very beginning of the design process. Even though lo-fab is an innovative approach to SID in and of itself, MASS took that one step further in their GHESKIO Cholera Treatment Center.[6] It would have been easy for the design firm to work out a building design that essentially replicated the typical building practices, methodologies, and materials of the local context, highlighting the admirable qualities and ignoring the least desirable ones.

Easy is rarely transformative.

---

4 See Chapter 4.
5 Bean. Interview with Mackenzy Vil.
6 MASS Design Group. "GHESKIO Cholera Treatment Center."

The design team chose to study deeper and discover a solution that would be not only culturally relevant and community driven but also intrinsically transformative. MASS reexamined the conditions of the soil in which they were to plant their work while simultaneously recognizing and celebrating the powerful tools they carried at their disposal, including complex digital design capabilities. Digital parametric design is a design methodology that employs algorithmic thinking to structure and configures the relationship between different design constraints and parameters (design intent) and their subsequent resulting form (design response).

In other words, math formulas turn data into shapes.

In the case of this specific project, the design team gathered numerous sources of data including local meteorology, patient spatial comfort and safety dimensions, and environmental context, then input that data into their parametric design software, manipulating and controlling it with their own design expertise in order to produce not only a functional building but also a design masterpiece. In 2014, the American Institute of Architects awarded this project with the AIA Knowledge Community Awards, calling the project "a culturally relevant response to specific community concerns that will have an impact far beyond the act of placing a healthcare building on a site."[7]

> *Easy is rarely transformative.*

In no way could this fantastic feat have been achieved if standard practice had been employed. Due to its nature of producing organic and more complex forms, industry standards have tried to limit parametric design to projects with bigger budgets from clients

---

7 MASS Design Group

with larger pocketbooks (for example, Frank Gehry's parametrically designed Guggenheim Museum in Bilbao, Spain, cost $340 a square foot, more than double the average cost of residential construction in the US).[8] Whether it be custom windows, wall panels, or any other building component uniquely begotten by means of parametric design, its powerful capacity has come to be harnessed in large part by the pragmatic master called economics.

Thanks in large part to the innovative vision of MASS to see this powerful tool enjoyed by both budget-heavy projects and SID, a bridge was formed between the typical and the ideal through the rejection of disregarding supposedly unattainable and inapplicable resources, replacing that limited mindset with a progressive and forward-thinking methodology. The result was a project that left the local Haitian community with a safe, efficient, and inspiring piece of architecture. Mackenzy Vil, the local craftsman who directed the construction of the building's unique metal panel façade, said, "When I finished, I realized it was art."[9]

STARchitects

The past century has seen a great deal of what many have termed "the STARchitect."[10] This term refers to those architects who have been widely recognized for their incredible design genius and their ability to create architecture that has become almost as much art as it is building. This international laud that has been bestowed upon such proclaimed architectural geniuses have become not only famous for their acts but also infamous for their character. Having gained a generalized reputa-

---

8 Wikipedia. "Guggenheim Museum Bilbao."
9 Bean
10 "Famous by Design"

tion for a pretentious attitude that cares less for the recipients of their work than how their work satisfies their artistic vision, these starchitects have received deafening applause and accolade in one ear while simultaneously enduring outbursts of disapproval and disgust in the other.

This, in large part, has led to a leap to the other end of the spectrum, resulting in the formation of a grassroots-focused, hyper-cultural respect design mentality. This approach to design proclaims the message of *human-centered design,** a phrase used to describe design that holistically integrates the opinions and desires of those who will actually inhabit and interact with the finished product.[11] Organizations like Rural Studio and the international design firm IDEO are strong proponents of this intentional reversal of design's often egotistical foundation, and they've seen amazing results. A

---

11 IDEO.org. *The Field Guide.*

quick perusal of Rural Studio's design portfolio will show you projects like their glass chapel, Hale County Animal Shelter, and countless residences that redefine beauty through the context of utmost interest and respect for colloquial ideologies, practices, and interests. I highly recommend all social entrepreneurs (specifically designers) read IDEO's *The Field Guide to Human-Centered Design*, or their current CEO and President Tim Brown's book *Change by Design*. Organizations such as these have always promoted a genuine and powerful interest in the value of design centered around those who will be most affected by its existence.

As with all good things, such a focus can unfortunately be misapplied in a way that disavows the need to continually pursue innovation in the field of social entrepreneurship.[12] When designers' unique and creative skills are ripped from the picture, hyper-cultural sensitivity is developed, and the possibility of applying innovative yet unfamiliar, "un-local" resources are shot down.

This has the potential to create an unmet need for innovation.

Instead, human-centered designers like MASS have shown the powerful way in which innovation can be integrated into colloquial design methodology. 100 Fold Studio Founder John Hudson promotes this same balance of local regionalism combined with outside expertise. He uses the phrase "experts and ambassadors" to describe this dichotomy. In the same way that MASS arrived at their design solutions for the Butaro District Hospital and Haiti Cholera Treatment Center through the synthesis of local understanding with their professional expertise, Hudson points to the importance of combining professional skill sets of so-called "experts"

---

12 This is a generalized statement and not a criticism of MASS or Rural Studio.

with the cumulative wisdom and understanding of local conditions held by local representatives of project sites, i.e., "ambassadors."[13] It is only by appreciating the value that each side has to bring to the table that the opposing dangers of irrelevant, egocentric monuments and weak, uninspired compromises may be avoided.

The Thorn and the Rose
What do Simprints, MASS Design Group, and Ashton Kutcher have in common? To answer that, we will first need to jump into a very dark but very serious problem the world faces today: child sex trafficking. In 1990, before the rise of the digital information, it was thought that child pornography was a dying issue. However, when technology allowed for imagery to be shared freely across the globe, the disease exploded from its death bed with increased ability to destroy the lives of countless children. Between 2004 and 2015, the number of sexual abuse files reviewed by the National Center for Missing and Exploited Children grew by more than 5,000 percent.[14] What was created to be a powerful tool for connecting the world had quickly revealed its sinister

13 John Hudson (Founder, 100 Fold Studio), interviewed by Jacob DeNeui in Battambang, Cambodia, July 14, 2017.
14 Thorn. "We are Thorn."

ability to create equally powerful pain and destruction.

That's when Thorn was born.

In 2009, after being deeply moved to respond to this crisis upon watching a documentary describing the issue of sex trafficking in Cambodia, actors Demi Moore and Ashton Kutcher created Thorn (then called DNA Foundation), an international anti-human trafficking organization that works to accelerate victim identification, deter abusers, and disrupt abuse platforms. Moore and Kutcher began by building a technology task force composed of some of the brightest minds in the tech industry to brainstorm and solve the daunting problem that lay before them. Through their efforts, tech moguls such as Google, Microsoft, Facebook, and Twitter lay aside their competitive attitudes and chose to come together on the issue. Thorn's CEO Julia Cordua states, "We are inspired, not deterred, by difficulty and we will continue to innovate, by bringing the best talent and resources to bear, to find children faster and stop abuse."[15]

One of their most powerful programs called "Shared Hash" serves as an example of Thorn's successful implementation of innovation in their work. When various internet content companies find pornographic images of children in their databases, through Shared Hash, they are then able to report that image to a cloud server, creating a digital fingerprint of that image. Then, when that image resurfaces on other networks, it becomes much easier to identify and prosecute the exploiter. "We have to stay on the cutting edge of that technology," co-founder Ashton Kutcher says, "because the criminals, they're on the cutting edge."[16]

In the same way that Simprints and MASS Design Group chose to embrace rather than fear the integra-

---

15 Cordua. "Defending Children From Sexual Abuse."
16 Thorn

tion of technology and innovation into the fabric of solving their unique social callings, Thorn has chosen to take the aggressive approach of radically employing the very best minds, tools, and programs in their quest to provide solutions for the problems that keep them up at night. These entities have demonstrated through their work that their cause is too important to be left in the incapable hands of outdated tools, methods, resources, and ways of thinking. Through their efforts, SID has radically shifted its strategy by moving from weak defense to a formidable offense, continually seeking to push the advantage against the different oppositions they have chosen to pour their life's work and creative prowess against. Whether it's bringing identity to billions of voiceless humans across the world, creating spaces that inspire and speak truth to mankind's inerrant self-worth, or defending the innocence of children across the digital landscape, these and other organizations have become examples of how social entrepreneurs can take back the power often removed from their arsenal by boldly stepping onto the field of the adjacent possible and operating in their fully empowered, innovative capacity.

> *"We have to stay on the cutting edge of that technology because the criminals, they're on the cutting edge."*
> - Ashton Kutcher

Power of the Tongue

Every social movement began with the awareness of a problem in the world followed by an insatiable desire to solve it. The seed of that movement most often originates in the heart and mind of an individual, but the eventual death or growth of that seed is almost completely dependent on one thing: human influences. An idea that is not acted upon is worth as much as this generation's future social security: nothing. Since the mind is designed to *form* ideas and not to *store* them, the biggest difference between successful social impact movements and the non-existent ones is that someone chose to act upon that idea they formed in their mind.

That's where human influences come in.

We live in a world that loves to squeeze the piss and vinegar out of every idealist who dares to describe aloud the dream he or she has of a better world, a vision that defies the mundane and exhaustive aspects of the socially crippled world in which we live. Perhaps it is shame that prompts those confined to the ground to shoot down any beautiful thing that flies, shame from the neglect of their own beautiful wings that could have propelled them into similar heights of glory but now, in their pitiful, atrophied state, are merely the burdensome blocks that hold them down and keep them from joining their flight-filled friends.

> *An idea that is not acted upon is worth as much as this generation's future social security: nothing.*

Disenchantment is a powerful enemy, and he hates to be alone. If you've ever sustained damage from a well-aimed shot of disenchantment, you know the devastating loss it produces. Whether it was an idea to turn social good into a profitable business or an aspiration to one day employ a currently non-existent technology to revolutionize the realm of social impact, many are the victim of this cold and efficient dream killer.

Armed with this weapon, human influence has too often acted as the guillotine to untold heads of beauty and transformation.

That very same human influence has also been the life blood to every, yes every, successful social entrepreneur's endeavor. As the Israelite King Solomon once said, "Death and life are in the power of the tongue". Ask any successful entrepreneur the story of his success. You need not wait long before they describe a person or network of people that inspired, enabled, and guided them in their pursuits towards success. Even Princess Diana of Wales has one such story.

> *Disenchantment is a powerful enemy, and he hates to be alone.*

Many will remember Princess Diana for her famed beauty and angst-ridden personal life. Some may know of her powerful influence in combatting the epidemic of AIDS through research, her care for people with leprosy, and the role she played in the abolition of the use of land mines. However, what many may not be aware of is the close yet unlikely friendship she shared with her social opposite: Mother Theresa.

In 1992, after a visit to Calcutta, India, to experience the incredible humanitarian work Mother Theresa was becoming so well known for, the princess described how that visit changed her life, providing her the direction she had sought for so many years. Between that introduction and her unfortunate death five years later, the two women would share numerous interactions with each other as well as undoubtedly countless amounts of deep inspiration. The princess' former butler Paul Burrell adds, "There's no doubt that this was the inspiration for all of the princess' wonderful humanitarian work."17

What is most inspiring about this story is the presence of the extreme hurdles and heartbreaks the princess endured along her journey. In 1996, she was divorced from her husband, Prince Charles, removing from her the official title as princess but not her resolve to fully utilize the impact of her great influence upon those in need, thanks in large part to the transformative effect a tiny Macedonian woman had on her passionate and caring soul.

The Web We Weave
Your social impact endeavor will either rise upon the shoulders of human influence or be crushed underneath its feet. People play the single most important role in determining whether one's seed of an idea will walk through the metamorphic process of development into mature life or instead suffer debilitating defeat. During the process of growth and struggle for any social impact endeavor, its story is seamlessly woven into the fabric of a network that is organically grown and developed over time. Each story is unique and essentially unpredictable, as is the way of all human interaction. If you look at any entrepreneur's journey, you'll discover a

17 Flood. "Prince

web of people that provided different areas of inspiration, expertise, and support for different purposes and at different times. The network that one creates along their entrepreneurial journey will undoubtedly come to support their work in numerous ways.

For Princess Diana, it was her connection to Mother Theresa that focused her life's energy and set her on the track to achieve what she had felt she was always meant to do. Undoubtedly the princess also likely took note of structures, systems, and other pragmatic elements of Mother Theresa's work that lent to her enormous impact as the princess visited Theresa's home in Calcutta and her convent in Rome.

Your social impact endeavor will either rise upon the shoulders of human influence or be crushed underneath its feet.

For MASS Design Group's Michael Murphy, the inspiration that would launch his future work in SID was already firmly set when he attended a lecture by Dr. Paul Farmer, the cofounder of Partners in Health. It was Murphy's connection with Dr. Farmer, however, that would lead to the first design project for both Murphy and cofounder Alan Ricks, the Butaro District Hospital in 2011. Without Dr. Farmer and his lecture on the sad state of buildings that were actually making people sicker in Rwanda, who knows how MASS would have achieved its jump start, or even if it would have.

For 100 Fold Studio, a critical part of their ability to focus more on their design work and less on the paper work attached to starting an international non-profit was their partnership to the international missionary training organization YWAM. Hudson approached YWAM and asked to be included as a subsidiary branch of the overall entity, giving them the freedom to fully operate under the legal 501(c)(3) status YWAM already had obtained until they were more fully equipped to achieve their own status. An additional benefit for 100 Fold Studio was YWAM's already vast and extensive network spread across the globe in countries such as Nepal, Bangladesh, and Cambodia. This global network has been the source of numerous initial projects for the design firm including their first built campus in Battambang, Cambodia.

No man is an island, and no social impact movement will ever grow into completion without the umbilical cord of human influence. Ideas, opportunities, and funding are all inextricably linked to the power of people and networks, so it is up to you, the designer, the entrepreneur, to approach this resource not as an unavoidable parasite on the back of your work but rather as an integral and life-giving source of value. And since we've already clarified the fact that you are indeed a designer, you must not forget to design. As we have seen, the formation story of everyone's network is completely different, so you can count on yours being different too.

Spaghetti Time
With so many possibilities and so many unknowns, where does one start? My suggestion is to start with the spaghetti phase (see Chapter 4). Attend lectures, read books, listen to podcasts. Seek to absorb as much content as possible. Sometimes, the best sources of inspiration are found outside of your field of interest. Even though I am an architect, in the past month of listening to TED talks I have exposed myself to count-

less thought-provoking topics such as Afrofuturism (a new wave of science fiction literature written through the lens of African authors), artificial intelligence, global warming, Creole cuisine, homelessness, and transgenderism.

In describing the importance of cross-industry innovation in an inspiration-driven economy, one source states, "Whereas the growth of our economy used to be determined by efficiency, these days it is mostly driven by inspiration and creativity... More and more companies are starting to realize the importance of translating knowledge and ideas from other companies, regions, or industries and applying them to products, processes, and business models within their own context."[18] Limiting yourself to the things that you would most often identify as direct interests may hinder your growth. This is just as true in SID as it is in business.

In our world of seemingly unlimited information, there is no excuse for not exposing ourselves to influences outside of our ordinary. One never knows where a certain connection will take you. It is both our privilege and our duty as social entrepreneurs to pursue diverse ways of thinking and understanding. Then, with your Crock-Pot full of collected ideas and inspirations, you can simultaneously experiment with various ideas and approaches to see

> *"Whereas the growth of our economy used to be determined by efficiency, these days it is mostly driven by inspiration and creativity."*
> - Bart Devoldere

---

18 Devoldere. "The Importance of Cross-Industry Innovation."

what sticks and what doesn't.

Time to Design
If you only walk in the footprints of those explorers who went before you, you will never reach an unreached summit. Use the stories of those who have inspired you as just that: inspiration. There is no such thing as a step-by-step guide to designing your resources, only a sea of hefty shoulders upon which to plant your feet so that you may gain previously unattainable positions of influence. Whether those resources you are designing are that of information and technology or of influence and networks, it will take the fullest and deepest application of your design capacity to accomplish this daunting feat. Neither the absence of technology and resources nor the sharpest arrows of disenchantment and negativity should keep you from scaling the fence that confines you to the world in which you live, a world you know you can improve. It's time to see the paper clip not as a hindrance but rather an unlocked possibility, a way to aid you in your fence-smashing ventures.

You're a designer, so it's time to design.

Chapter 8 in a page...

- Creativity is simply the ability to identify patterns.
- The application of new construction technology in the Roman insula tangibly demonstrates that ancient Rome believed people matter, regardless of economic status.
- Simprints's advancements in biometric technology demonstrates that social entrepreneurs can be on the cutting edge of the adjacent possible.
- Through MASS Design Group's Lo-Fab principle, the firm is not only able to insource sustainable building trades but also do so through the innovative application of digital parametric design.
- The "expert and ambassador" concept teaches the wisdom in balancing the collective merit of the professional "expert" and local "ambassador."
- Every SID endeavor succeeds or fails in part due to the social network they create.
- Expose yourself to new people, ideas, and technology in order to discover the spark that will propel your endeavor forward.

Food for Thought...

1. What's one tool that you think would be impossible to ever employ in your social impact organization? Now think of ways you could sustainably incorporate it into your arsenal of tools.
2. Think about the "expert and ambassador" scale. Which end of the spectrum would you say you lean? What would it look like to achieve a better "tension" between the two?
3. Come up with the names of five to twenty (depending on how ambitious you are) people that you look up to, whether or not you share the same industry. Contact them and either ask for advice, propose an idea that might benefit them, or simply encourage them by letting them know how much they have impacted you. They may not reply, but you'll never know unless you try!

CONCLUSION

"If you wait for all the lights to turn green before starting your journey, you'll never leave the driveway."

- Zig Ziglar

Drones Saves Lives

She had no idea how close she would come to losing her life that day.

While giving birth via C-section, a twenty-four-year-old Rwandan woman began to hemorrhage severely. The doctors tried to replace the blood she had lost but were limited to the merely two units of her blood type that they had on hand. In an attempt to save her life, one of the doctors pulled out his phone, sent a text, and within ten minutes a small, autonomous drone flying at 100 kilometers an hour deposited a small cardboard container filled with more of the life-saving blood this woman needed to survive her tumultuous delivery. Seven units of blood cells, four units of plasma, and two units of platelets later (more blood than you contain in your entire body), the doctors were able to stabilize the woman, saving both her and her baby.

So how was it that a tiny flying machine in the middle of East Africa, of all places, was able to be the deciding factor between life and death for this young mother? That's a question that young entrepreneur

Keller Rinaudo, CEO of the new Rwandan-based company Zipline decided to answer. In 2014, Rinaudo launched Zipline with the cross-cultural belief that innovative, profitable business could and should take place in Africa, saying: "Most people think that new technology or advanced technology can never start in Africa. Instead, they think that the best way to help the continent advance is by providing aid or services that the continent can't provide for itself. That attitude couldn't be more wrong."[1] As a robotics entrepreneur, Rinaudo set out to design a business built around an electric autonomous air delivery system that could help solve Rwanda's (and someday even the world's) difficulty in safe and sustainable blood storage and transportation.

Keeping adequate supplies of blood on hand at hospitals and health centers is a challenge not only for Rwanda but for every country. Blood has a short shelf life, numerous storage requirements, and is extremely difficult to predict demand. Those who work with blood know how hard it is to keep an adequate amount on hand. Too much blood and one inherently creates more waste; too little and doctors are ill-equipped to handle patients' needs.

In 2016, Zipline launched the very first automated blood delivery system in the world to operate at national scale due to the forward thinking of Rwandan President Paul Kagame and the Rwandan Ministry of Health. Zipline now delivers 20 percent of the nation's blood supply to about twelve hospitals (that's somewhere between 12,000-16,000 units of blood).[2] Countless patients in Rwanda in need of blood transfusions, just like with the twenty-four-year-old mother whose life was in danger, are now experiencing the benefits of one of the—if

---

1 Rinaudo. "How We're Using Drones."
2 Rinaudo

not *the*—world's most innovative and effective remote blood transportation system.

When the doctor sent that text message, he was communicating to Zipline their immediate need for blood. Zipline was then able to pull the exact amount needed from the National Center for Blood Transfusion, scan the blood into their system, then shoot it off in one of their autonomous drones where it was then dropped via paper parachute ("simple things are best" says Rinaudo)[3] onto a designated landing pad, safely, quickly, and efficiently.

Innovation's Mecca
Silicon Valley and technology. Portland and coffee. New York City and commerce. When you think of one, you often think of the other. That's because each of these cities has become known as a breeding ground for creativity and innovation in their respective field.

And now the whole world knows it.

Anyone interested in creating a tech startup knows that the greatest cluster of inspiration, funding, and possibility in the US currently lies in the Silicon Valley, and one will most likely achieve the greatest odds of success in their tech startup by immersing themselves within this pool of opportunity. This hub of innovativeness inherently creates a self-sustaining life force of ever-evolving, ever-growing sparks of opportunity. As more and more boundaries are pushed within technology in the Silicon Valley, the more and more that area will sharpen its edge in a world where technology is changing faster than the blink of an eye.

Organizations like Zipline, and all of the examples we have explored in this book, give me hope that one day social impact organizations can become known as

3 Rinaudo

the mecca of innovation in numerous fields. The Earth may still be spinning at the same speed it was fifty years ago, but society is progressing at an ever-accelerated rate, giving us new insights and perspectives regarding the role of social entrepreneurship in the world. David Dewane, former Editor in Chief at Impact Design Hub, says this: "We're in a transitionary moment where what has been talked about in public interest design was charity. We were in a cheerleading phase where any project that got built was talked about and everyone was nice to one another. Those days are over."[4] We are beyond the point of being satisfied with good intentions. Now is the time for social entrepreneurs in every industry to step up their game, to innovate better and more effective organization structures in order to deliver better and more efficient work.

And the whole world needs it.

If meeting the world's greatest and deepest needs is a value the world as a collective holds dear, why are there not more entrepreneurs like Keller Rinaudo, John Hudson, and Liz Bohannon challenging our paradigms of how social impact is to be achieved today?

In Summary...

Our fable of the three explorers and how their unique choices influenced the success of their endeavors gave us an alternative way to view the role design innovation plays in getting where we want to go, which in

> *Social impact ogranizations can become known as the mecca of innovation in numerous fields.*

---

[4] David Dewane, interviewed by Jacob DeNeui, June 28, 2017.

our case is greater effectiveness. (If design is the tracks which guide and empower the engine of innovation, effectiveness is innovation's destination.) Peter, Will, and Sid were unexpectedly thrown into a great debacle when their Mysterious Island decided to get a little jiggy and ruin their plans for a manageable feat of safe and enjoyable exploration. The avalanche forced them to respond to a challenge far greater than anything they had ever experienced before. Even though all three were simultaneously thrown into the same sticky mess of finding means of reunion and rescue with their other partners, they each went about answering the call to act in a different way.

    Peter, in all of his strength and focus, chose the decisive yet tragically oblivious response, resulting in a conclusion that took him in a completely different direction from where he wanted to go. Will, with his calm yet narrow-minded reasoning, was unable to overcome a failed beginning strategy, leading him to a place he had inaccurately pinned as his desired destination. And atop the mountain, left alone to think through her strategy with nothing but a faint yet pulsating feeling of passion and conviction to discover truths perhaps not yet revealed, Sid stood as the metaphorical enigma of what exciting possibilities lie in wait for you when careful forethought is given to how innovation can become, more integrated into the formation, business models and overarching structures of your social impact organization.

    We then examined Blockbuster, Kmart, and Yellow Cab and saw that **innovation** within an industry is often a key predictor in determining whether an organization will thrive or slowly shrink into obscurity. With the ever-increasing need for design innovation due to forces such as war, environmental instability, and increased population growth, the need for social entrepreneurs to step up their "A" game has and will only continue to increase in the foreseeable future. The only way for this predicted increase in demand to be met is for innovation to become an integral component of your social impact world.

In Chapter 5, I shared three design basics that can help any social entrepreneur innovate how they approach the formation of their organization. First, we learned how to distinguish between the **problem** and the **need**. If you are to be an effective social entrepreneur, you must learn to identify the objective gap that you are trying to fill while ignoring pre-conceived (and likely false) notions about what the solution to that gap might be. Next, we looked at turning **roadblocks** into **opportunities**. Too often we either treat the obstacles in our way as a battering ram as we try to force solutions that will never work or we give up instead of finding a creative and innovative approach to overcoming the obstacle. Finally, we looked at how to **explore** before **committing**. This will be a balancing act of both avoiding the "straddling" of multiple incongruent ideas while simultaneously giving yourself the freedom to explore ideas that may perhaps even originate from outside of your field of work.

In the final three chapters, we looked at some tangible examples of several areas which I have identified as the most prevalent fields of innovation within social entrepreneurship currently, including Purpose, Funding, and Resources—illustrated through 100 Fold Studio, Grameen Bank, and Thorn. These organizations are actively pushing the boundary of the adjacent possible, each in their own way, bringing light and hope to the world while proving that innovation can and is happening within social impact organizations.

Isirika

In Western Kenya, there is a tribe known as the Maragoli. Embedded in the Maragoli culture is a philosophy and way of life known as "isirika*," a pragmatic way of producing equality and mutual benefit for everyone through means of charity, philanthropy, and service.[5] When one village member is sick and unable to plow their fields, neighbors come together in support. To afford children the costly privilege of attending school, the whole community combines their financial resources to fund the child's education. When community issues such as health, building, and planting crops arise, the people assemble in order to develop solutions.

At first glance, this African practice might appear to be nothing more than basic social welfare, yet it is so much more. "Isirika affirms common humanity," says Kenyan human rights advocate Musimbi Kanyoro. "When you begin that you're human together, you see each other differently. You don't see a refugee first and you don't see a woman first and you don't see a person with disability first. You see a human being first."[6] Our world is in need of isirika and is desperate for solutions to real problems requiring real solutions—solutions that innovative design has the power to produce.

If you're reading this book, you either know my mom or have some level of interest in social impact work and its ability to meet the deepest needs our world faces. By preemptively applying the concepts from this book to the design and construction of your social impact organizations before embarking upon your unique work, in other words "designing before you design," there is no limit to what you can achieve. There

---

5 Kanyoro. "To Solve the World's Biggest Problems."
6 Kanyoro

is no problem you cannot solve. There is no obstacle you cannot overcome.

People Matter
Great possibilities lie behind us through history's wisdom, beside us through our current comrades, and before us through untapped design potential. I see a brave new world and a future where social entrepreneurship is empowered by innovation to solve problems, meet needs, and most importantly, remind us of our humanity, our worth, and the common bond we all share. I see a world where design stands as a common battle cry, a banner to be waved against the tyrannies of war, sickness, and injustice, foes that may perhaps strike terror in the heart of some but who will fare poorly against the power of design when wielded by creative and innovative social entrepreneurs. I see a world where designers like you and me begin to believe that the conceptual platforms and organizational structures within which design is allowed to cultivate solutions can actually be intentionally formed and designed in order to propel social impact fields as a whole from a state of "surviving" to "thriving." If this world is to become a reality, we must refuse to lose our initial idealism that gave us the hope to dream about what social impact organizations could become.

> *"When you begin that you're human together, you see each other differently."*
> *- Musimbi Kanyoro*

Above all, we must remember one thing:

People matter.

ACKNOWLEDGEMENTS

There are so many people that helped make this book possible. To my family, thank you for empowering me to believe I could do anything. Your encouragement and support means the world to me.

John Hudson, thank you for your investment in me and showing me there was a different way to do architecture. Thank you also for taking the time to provide input for the content of this book.

Lindsay Schack, thank you for taking the time to read my manuscript and help me refocus the book. It turned out so much better because of you!

David Dewane, thank you for responding to an anonymous email and letting me interview you. Your sacrifice of time is so appreciated.

David Yakos, thanks for drawing pictures for me while sitting on a seat in the sky.

Caleb Walker, thank you for sharing your time with me and letting me learn more about your inspiring business. I'm glad we're friends now.

Alora Boerner, your meticulous eye for detail and depth of literary knowledge made this book so much cleaner and more polished.

Tera, you inspire me to be a better writer and a better person. Thank you for living fearlessly in all that you do!

And finally, a HUGE thank you to my launch team: Manfred Jeske, David Boye, Mahelet Kassa,

David Reimer, Mike Reimer, Brian Grasso, Sarah Pettigrew, Houston Abbott, and several others. Without you, nobody would have heard of this book.

GLOSSARY

- **501(c)(3)**
    - The portion of the US Internal Revenue Code that allows for federal tax exemption of non-profit organizations, specifically those that are considered public charities, private foundations, or private operating foundations
- **Adjacent Possible**
    - The region just beyond what is currently cutting edge
- **Benefit Corporation (B-Corp)**
    - A for-profit company certified by the non-profit B Lab to meet rigorous standards of social and environmental performance, accountability, and transparency
- **Creativity**
    - The process of conceiving new ideas through the synthesis of raw information
- **Design**
    - The intentional process by which an original physical, digital, or intellectual product is created
    - Design uses **creativity** to produce **subjective** benefits

- **Digital Age (aka Computer Age, Information Age, or New Media Age)**
  - *The period of time starting anywhere from the mid 1950s to late 1970s until now, characterized by the adoption and proliferation of digital computers*
- **Double Bottom Line**
  - *A way of measuring success by factoring both fiscal performance – through financial profit and loss analysis – as well as positive social impact*
- **Human-Centered Design**
  - *Design produced in response to direct observation of the needs and desires of the design's recipient(s)*
- **Humanitarian Design**
  - *The intentional creation of physical, digital, or intellectual material for the purpose of reducing human suffering and inequality*
- **Industrial Age**
  - *The period of time between the mid 18th century and late 20th century which experienced significant change in social and economic* organization resulting from the *replacement* of *hand tools* by machine and power tools and the *development* of *large-scale industrial production*
- **Information Age**
  - *Sometimes synonymous with the "Digital Age" but more accurately describes the modern age, regarded as a time in which information has become a commodity that is quickly and widely disseminated and easily available especially through the use of computer technology*

- **Innovation**
    - *The introduction of something new*
    - *Innovation uses **creativity** to produce **objective** benefits*
- **Isirika**
    - *A philosophy and way of life from the western Kenyan Maragoli tribe describing a pragmatic way of producing equality and mutual benefit for everyone through means of charity, philanthropy, and service*
- **Non-Government Organization (NGO)**
    - *Autonomous entities which typically exist for the promotion of philanthropic causes such as health, education, and human rights*
- **Non-Profit**
    - *A corporation or an association that conducts business for the benefit of the general public without shareholders and without a profit motive (see 501(c)(3))*
- **Philanthropy**
    - *goodwill to fellow members of the human race; especially : active effort to promote human welfare*
- **Pro Bono**
    - *Denoting work undertaken without charge, especially legal work for a client with a low income*
- **Social Entrepreneurship**
    - *The application of business and/or organization start-ups toward addressing social, cultural, and/or environmental needs; performance is commonly measured by "positive influence" upon society as opposed to more common business metrics such as profit and loss*

- **Social Impact Design/Impact Design (SID)**
  - *Design that produces positive change by respecting the dignity and value of humanity through the partnership between a design field and an altruistic cause*
- **Zeitgeist**
  - *The defining spirit or mood of a particular period of history as shown by the ideas and beliefs of the time*

BIBLIOGRAPHY

Abrahamson, Eric John. *Beyond Charity: A Century of Philanthropic Innovation*. Rockefeller Foundation, 2013.

AIANational. "An Architect's Story: Chris Downey." YouTube video, 3:40. Published on May 15, 2015. https://www.youtube.com/watch?v=zrtfXDk0L8A.

Bean, Thatcher. Interview with Mackenzy Vil. "Mackenzy Vil: The LoFab Movement." MASS Design Group video, 4:09. 2014. massdesigngroup.org/videos.

Becker, Jeffrey A. "Roman Domestic Architecture (insula)." Khan Academy, n.d. https://www.khanacademy.org/humanities/ancient-art-civilizations/roman/beginners-guide-rome/a/roman-domestic-architecture-insula.

"Bill and Melinda Gates Foundation." Influence Watch, n.d. https://www.influencewatch.org/non-profit/bill-and-melinda-gates-foundation/.

B Lab. "Year in Review: The B Corp Impact in 2017." B the Change, December 28, 2017. https://bthechange.com/year-in-review-the-b-corp-impact-in-2017-f529a229921f.

Bodnar, Matt. Interview with Beth Comstock. "You Can Become More Creative With This Unique Strategy Used By American Spies with Beth Comstock." *The Science of Success*. Podcast audio, January 31, 2019. https://www.successpodcast.com/show-notes/2019/1/30/you-can-become-more-creative-with-this-unique-strategy-used-by-american-spies-with-beth-comstock.

Brown, Tim, and Barry Katz. *Change by Design: How Design Thinking Transforms Organizations and Inspires Innovation*. Harper Collins, 2009.

Carnoy, Martin, and Emma Garcia. "Five Key Trends in U.S. Student Performance: Progress by Blacks and Hispanics, the Takeoff of Asians, the Stall of Non-English Speakers, the Persistence of Socioeconomic Gaps, and the Damaging Effect of Highly Segregated Schools." Economic Policy Institute, January 12, 2017. www.epi.org/publication/five-key-trends-in-u-s-student-performance-progress-by-blacks-and-hispanics-the-takeoff-of-asians-the-stall-of-non-english-speakers-the-persistence-of-socioeconomic-gaps-and-the-damaging-effect/.

Cary, John. *The Power of Pro Bono: 40 Stories about Design for the Public Good by Architects and Their Clients*. Metropolis Books, 2010.

"Charitable Contributions You Think You Can Claim but Can't." Intuit TurboTax, 2018. https://turbotax.intuit.com/tax-tips/charitable-contributions/charitable-contributions-you-think-you-can-claim-but-cant/L2XxnoskD.

"Children: Reducing Mortality." World Health Organization, September 19, 2018. https://www.who.int/news-room/fact-sheets/detail/children-reducing-mortality.

Coan, Hannah, and Dana Schwartz. "Millennials Demand More From Employers and Investments." Capital Group, August 29, 2017. www.capitalgroup.com/our-company/news-room/milliennials-demand-more-from-employers-investments.html.

Cohen, Reuven. "Business Success Is Happening Faster Than Ever, But So Is Failure. How to Adapt." Wired, August 7, 2015. www.wired.com/insights/2014/05/business-success-happening-faster-ever-failure-adapt/.

Coleman, Ken. Interview with Bobby Gruenewald. "#287: Bobby Gruenewald—Find a Way, Not an Excuse." *The EntreLeadership Podcast*. Podcast audio, 2018. https://www.entreleadership.com/blog/podcasts/bobby-gruenewald.

Coleman, Ken. Interview with Charles Duhigg. "#286: Charles Duhigg—Ignore Conventional Wisdom." *The EntreLeadership Podcast*. Podcast audio, 2018. https://www.entreleadership.com/blog/podcasts/charles-duhigg.

Coleman, Ken. Interview with Zoro the Drummer. "#207: Zoro the Drummer—Why the World Needs Your Gifts." *The EntreLeadership Podcast*. Podcast audio, 2017. https://www.entreleadership.com/blog/podcasts/zoro-drummer-world-needs-gifts.

Company Man. "The Decline of Blockbuster...What Happened?" YouTube video, 12:42. Published June 21, 2017. https://

www.youtube.com/watch?v=5sMXR7rK40U.

Company Man. "The Decline of Kmart...What Happened?" YouTube video, 13:49. Published May 15, 2017. https://www.youtube.com/watch?v=1__Qg1toSSs.

Cordua, Julia. "Defending Children From Sexual Abuse | About Thorn." Thorn. www.wearethorn.org/about-our-fight-against-sexual-exploitation-of-children/.

Desilver, Drew. "Despite Concerns about Global Democracy, Nearly Six-in-Ten Countries Are Now Democratic." Pew Research Center, December 6, 2017. http://www.pewresearch.org/fact-tank/2017/12/06/despite-concerns-about-global-democracy-nearly-six-in-ten-countries-are-now-democratic/.

Devoldere, Bart. "The Importance of Cross-Industry Innovation in an Inspiration-Driven Economy." Vlerick Business School, June 24, 2016. www.vlerick.com/en/research-and-faculty/knowledge-items/knowledge/the-importance-of-cross-industry-innovation-in-an-inspiration-driven-economy.

Downey, Chris. "Design with the Blind in Mind." Filmed October 2013. TED video, 11:36. https://www.ted.com/talks/chris_downey_design_with_the_blind_in_mind/up-next#t-156444.

Flood, Rebecca. "Princess Diana Found Her 'Calling' Following Spiritual Meeting with Mother Teresa." *Express Newspapers*, August 21, 2017. www.express.co.uk/news/world/844100/Princess-Diana-mother-Teresa-spiritual-calling-meeting-Paul-Burrell.

"Global Estimates on Modern Slavery: Forced Labour and Forced Marriage." International Labour Office and Walk Free Foundation, in partnership with International Organization for Migration, September 19, 2017. https://www.ilo.org/global/publications/books/WCMS_575479/lang--en/index.htm.

Hartmans, Avery, and Nathan McAlone. "The Story of How Travis Kalanick Built Uber into the Most Feared and Valuable Start-up in the World." Business Insider, August 1, 2016. https://www.businessinsider.com/ubers-history.

Hyams, Joe. *Zen in the Martial Arts*. Bantam, 1997.

IDEO.org. *The Field Guide to Human-Centered Design*. IDEO.org, 2015.

Interview with Mia Scharpie. "The Fun Palace 014: Mia Scharphie." ImpactDesignHub.com. *The Fun Palace Podcast*. Podcast audio, July 10, 2017. https://player.fm/series/impact-design-hub/the-fun-palace-014-mia-scharphie.

Kanyoro, Musimbi. "To Solve the World's Biggest Problems, Invest in Women and Girls." Filmed November 2017. TED video, 14:30. www.ted.com/talks/musimbi_kanyoro_to_solve_the_world_s_biggest_problems_invest_in_women_and_girls.

Kaufholz, Eddie. Interview with Liz Forkin Bohannon." Liz Forkin Bohannon, Founder of Sseko Designs." *The New Activist*. Podcast audio, November 2, 2017. https://www.stitcher.com/podcast/the-new-activist/e/52085108.

King, Stephen. *On Writing: A Memoir of the Craft*. Hodder, 2012.

Kleon, Austin. *Steal like an Artist: 10 Things Nobody Told You about Being Creative*. Workman, 2012.

Lewis, Kern. "Kmart's Ten Deadly Sins." *Forbes Magazine*, June 6, 2013. https://www.forbes.com/2003/10/10/1010kmartreview.html#dffee911aa1e.

Male, Richard. "Nonprofit Weaknesses Start With Too Few Leaders and Too Many Managers." Chronicle of Philanthropy, February 10, 2013. https://www.philanthropy.com/article/Nonprofit-Weaknesses-Start/155399.

Manhart, Sebastian, and Emma Millar. "Building a Social Enterprise: The Legal Landscape." Simprints Technology - Resources, 2018. https://uploads-ssl.webflow.com/5a0ad2cbd65a2f-0001be3903/5ba1f16dacf579565fdf356d_SimPrints-Building-a-Social-Enterprise.pdf.

Marshall, Andrew C. "There's A Critical Difference Between Creativity And Innovation." Business Insider, April 10, 2013. www.businessinsider.com/difference-between-creativity-and-innovation-2013-4.

MASS Design Group. "GHESKIO Cholera Treatment Center." *Architect Magazine*, August 8, 2014. www.architectmagazine.com/project-gallery/gheskio-cholera-treatment-center.

Matulka, Rebecca. "Timeline: History of the Electric Car." Energy.gov, September 15, 2014. https://www.energy.gov/articles/history-electric-car.

McMillon, Doug. "We're Updating Our Legal Name to Reflect How Customers Want to Shop - Here's Why." Walmart Today, December 6, 2017. https://blog.walmart.com/business/20171206/were-updating-our-legal-name-to-reflect-how-customers-want-to-shop-heres-why.

"Monthly Report: 2019-01 Issue 469 in USD" Grameen Bank, "February 13, 2019." http://www.grameen.com/monthly-report-2019-01-issue-469-in-usd/

"Netflix – Overview - Profile." Netflix Investors. https://www.netflix-investor.com/ir-overview/profile/default.aspx.

Offit, Paul A., reviewer. "Global Immunization: Worldwide Disease Incidence." Children's Hospital of Philadelphia, reviewed on March 28, 2018. https://www.chop.edu/centers-programs/vaccine-education-center/global-immunization/diseases-and-vaccines-world-view.

Oremus, Will. "The End of the Taxi Era." *Slate Magazine*, January 8, 2016. www.slate.com/articles/technology/technology/2016/01/yellow_cab_in_san_francisco_is_just_the_beginning_uber_s_war_on_cabs_is.html.

"Our Story – The BioLite History and Team." BioLite. https://www.bioliteenergy.com/pages/our-story.

Parvin, Alastair. "Architecture for the People by the People." Filmed February 2013. TED video, 13:08. www.ted.com/talks/alastair_parvin_architecture_for_the_people_by_the_people.

Patterson, Kerry, Joseph Grenny, David Maxfield, Ron McMillan, and Al Switzler. *Influencer: The Power to Change Anything*. McGraw-Hill, 2007.

Peterson, John. "Public Architecture » AboutPublic Architecture." Public Architecture. www.publicarchitecture.org/about/.

Petrilla, Molly. "'Millennipreneurs' Are Starting More Businesses, Targeting Higher Profits." *Fortune*, February 20, 2016. http://fortune.com/2016/02/20/millennial-entrepreneurs-study/.

Phillips, Matt, and Roberto A. Ferdman. "A Brief, Illustrated History of Blockbuster, which Is Closing the Last of Its US Stores." Quartz, November 6, 2013. https://qz.com/144372/a-brief-illustrated-history-of-blockbuster-which-is-closing-the-last-of-its-us-stores/.

Pinker, Steven. "Is the World Getting Better or Worse? A Look at the Numbers." Filmed April 2018. TED video, 18:33. www.ted.com/talks/steven_pinker_is_the_world_getting_better_or_worse_a_look_at_the_numbers.

Porter, Michael E., and Mark R. Kramer. "The Competitive Advantage of Corporate Philanthropy." *Harvard Business Review*, August 1, 2014. hbr.org/2002/12/the-competitive-advantage-of-corporate-philanthropy.

Quirk, Vanessa. "Introducing 'Potty-Girl,' The Architect of the Future?" ArchDaily, July 24, 2014. www.archdaily.com/529934/introducing-potty-girl-the-architect-of-the-future.

Rinaudo, Keller. "How We're Using Drones to Deliver Blood and Save Lives." Filmed August 2017. TED video, 15:31. www.ted.com/talks/keller_rinaudo_how_we_re_using_drones_to_deliver_blood_and_save_lives.

Ritholtz, Barry. "The Pace of Innovation and Disruption Is Accelerating." The Big Picture, July 6, 2017. https://ritholtz.com/2017/07/pace-innovation-disruption-accelerating/.

Satell, Greg. "A Look Back At Why Blockbuster Really Failed And Why It Didn't Have To." *Forbes Magazine*, September 21, 2014. www.forbes.com/sites/gregsatell/2014/09/05/a-look-back-at-why-blockbuster-really-failed-and-why-it-didnt-have-to/.

Simpson, Campbell. "The Tesla Model S 'Skateboard' Rolling Chassis Is a Thing of Beauty." Gizmodo, December 9, 2014. https://www.gizmodo.com.au/2014/12/the-tesla-model-s-skateboard-rolling-chassis-is-a-thing-of-beauty/.

Sinclair, Cameron. "My Wish: A Call for Open-Source Architecture." Filmed February 2006. TED video, 22:25. www.ted.com/talks/cameron_sinclair_on_open_source_architecture.

"Sseko Designs's Competitors, Revenue, Number of Employees, Funding and Acquisitions." Owler, n.d. https://www.owler.com/company/ssekodesigns.

Stephens, Philip. "State versus Citizen in Tomorrow's World." Financial Times, December 13, 2012. https://www.ft.com/content/75dfa02c-448d-11e2-932a-00144feabdc0.

Taylor-Hochberg, Amelia. Interview with Garrett Jacobs. "One-to-One #11 with Garrett Jacobs." *Archinect Sessions*. Podcast audio, February 17, 2016. iTunes.

TED. "Architecture That's Built to Heal | Michael Murphy." YouTube video, 15:38. Published October 6, 2016. https://www.youtube.com/watch?v=MvXZzKZ3JYQ.

TEDx Talks. "A History of Microfinance | Muhammad Yunus | TedxVienna." YouTube video, 23:46. Published January 18, 2012. www.youtube.com/watch?v=6UCuWxWiMaQ.

TEDx Talks. "What the World Doesn't Need Is Another Non-Profit | John Levy | TEDxAmherstCollege." YouTube video, 17:23. Published December 18, 2014. www.youtube.com/watch?v=gslCOrmlVuk.

"Tegu's Competitors, Revenue, Number of Employees, Funding and Acquisitions." Owler, n.d. https://www.owler.com/company/tegu.

The New York Times Conferences. "Infrastructure with Bjarke Ingels." YouTube video, 51:59. Published July 21, 2015. www.youtube.com/watch?v=eizyClsZutM.

Thorn. "We are Thorn." YouTube video, 6:35. Published November 14, 2013. www.youtube.com/watch?time_continue=9&v=Se-4OvAGJu4U.

Vlaskovits, Patrick. "Henry Ford, Innovation, and That 'Faster Horse' Quote." Harvard Business Review, August 29, 2011. https://hbr.org/2011/08/henry-ford-never-said-the-fast.

Wallace, Tracey. "New Report Proves Unanimous Agreement: Fast Fashion Spurs Need for Change in the Fashion Industry." BigCommerce, n.d. https://www.bigcommerce.com/blog/new-report-proves-unanimous-agreement-time-ripe-change-fashion-industry/#undefined.

Wikipedia contributors. "Guggenheim Museum Bilbao." Wikipedia, The Free Encyclopedia. https://en.wikipedia.org/w/index.php?title=Guggenheim_Museum_Bilbao&oldid=883784510.

Wikipedia contributors. "List of Ongoing Armed Conflicts," Wikipedia, The Free Encyclopedia. https://en.wikipedia.org/w/index.php?title=List_of_ongoing_armed_conflicts&oldid=884012766.

Wood, Hannah. "Emergency Shelter: Housing for the Age of Mass Displacement." Archinect, July 20, 2017. archinect.com/features/article/150018423/emergency-shelter-housing-for-the-age-of-mass-displacement.

Woods, Wendy. "The Business Benefits of Doing Good." Filmed October 2017. TED video, 15:36. www.ted.com/talks/wendy_woods_the_business_benefits_of_doing_good.

LET'S START A
CONVERSATION

I want to hear from YOU about the social impact YOU are making!

#DesginBeforeYouDesign

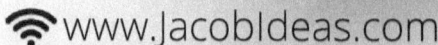 www.JacobIdeas.com
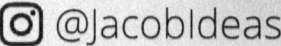 @JacobIdeas
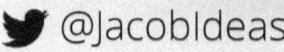 @JacobIdeas

www.ingramcontent.com/pod-product-compliance
Lightning Source LLC
Chambersburg PA
CBHW030615220526
45463CB00004B/1294